The Narcissist's Daughter

From Breakdown to Breakthrough

Kylie B

© 2024 The Narcissist's Daughter by Kylie B. All rights reserved
Cover Design by Valentina Zagaglia

No part of this publication may be reproduced, distributed, or transmitted in any form or by any means, including photocopying, recording, or other electronic or mechanical methods, without the prior written permission of the publisher, except in the case of brief quotations embodied in critical reviews and certain other non-commercial uses permitted by copyright law.

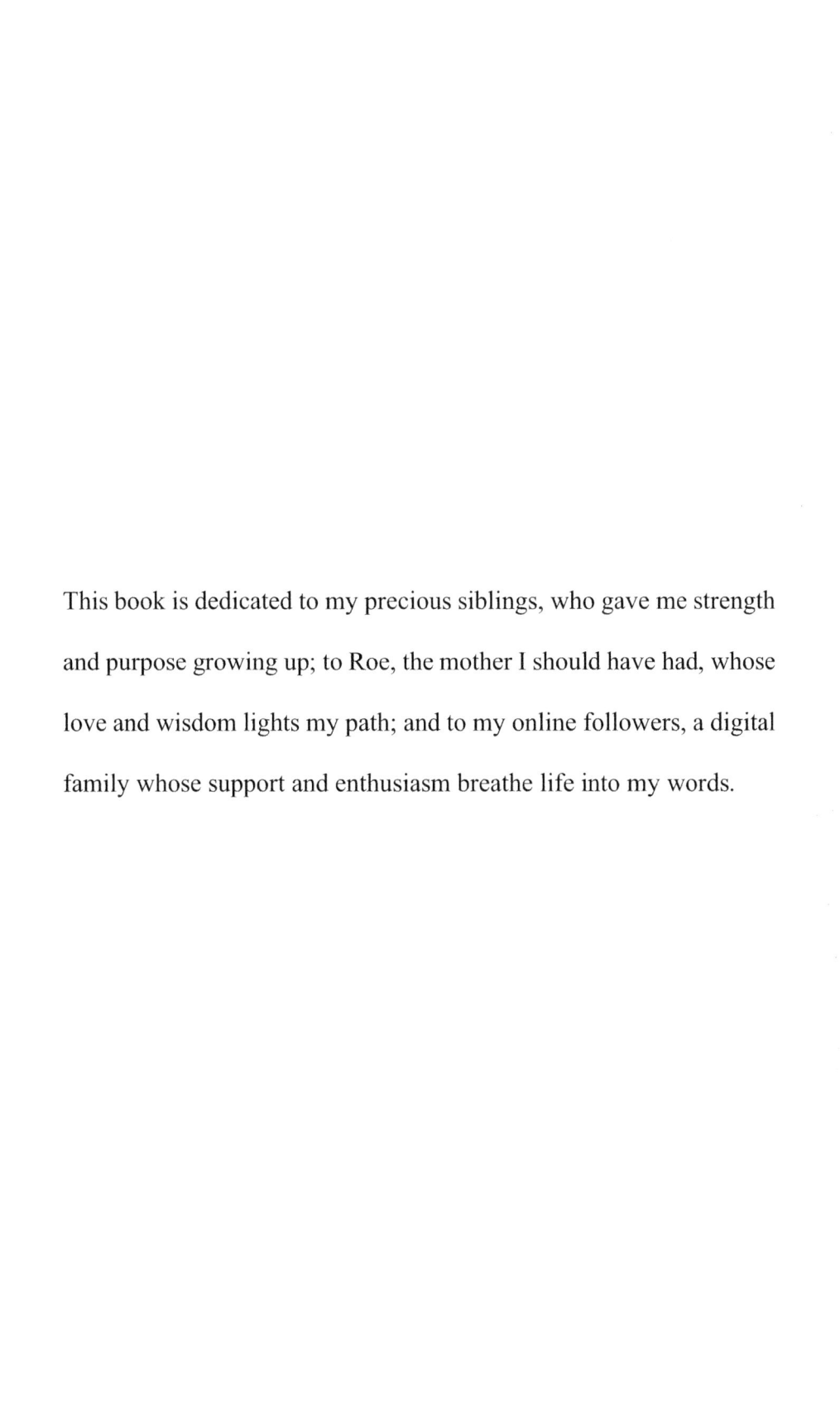

This book is dedicated to my precious siblings, who gave me strength and purpose growing up; to Roe, the mother I should have had, whose love and wisdom lights my path; and to my online followers, a digital family whose support and enthusiasm breathe life into my words.

Acknowledgements:

What an incredible journey it has been bringing this book to life. After a decade in the making, I am so grateful to finally share my story. However, this achievement wouldn't have been possible without the support of a few remarkable individuals along the way.

First off, big love to my siblings. You guys gave me the strength to power through growing up. Knowing you were looking up to me kept me going, and turning my pain into my superpower was all thanks to you. Your trust in me and your dependence on my guidance, fuelled a determination within me to rise above my own struggles and be a source of comfort and inspiration for you.

This isn't just my story- it is a collective story that weaved the threads of our lives together. Your influence and presence shaped not only my journey but also the essence of who I am. In every endeavour, every triumph, and every setback, you were the silent force driving me forward.

Acknowledging your impact on my life is an acknowledgment of our shared experiences, our shared triumphs, and our shared struggles. So, like I said, this story isn't mine alone; it belongs to you as well. Every step of the way, everything I have ever done, every challenge I've faced, and every success I've celebrated – it has all been for you.

So, my siblings, you are more than just family; you are my co-authors and my fellow travellers on this journey called life. Your influence is etched into the very core of this story, and I am extremely grateful for the strength and purpose you've infused into my life.

Now, a special acknowledgment is reserved for the remarkable woman, Roe. Recognising your impact on my life requires a heartfelt expression of the intense gratitude and deep connection I feel toward you. Roe, you are the example of unwavering support and the definition of a mother's love. In a world where the concept of family can be complex, you seamlessly walked into my life and chose to be a steady presence. Your decision to embrace me as your own highlights the beauty of chosen family. While you may not have given me the gift of life, life, in turn, gave me the unmatched gift of you.

Your role in shaping my identity and guiding me toward the best version of myself is endless. Your support has been a constant source of strength, guiding me forward during times of uncertainty and challenge. Through your actions and the love you've generously shared, you've taught me what it means to be a lovable daughter, and provided a foundation for a deep sense of belonging.

Expressing the depth of my gratitude is hard, as words seem inadequate to capture the enormity of the emotions involved. You mean more to me than can be articulated, and your influence has become an important part of who I am.

As I navigate through life, I hope I continue to make you proud. The love and affection I hold for you go beyond the ordinary, exceeding into a realm where you are not just a figure in my life but an integral part of my heart.

So, thank you for being my guiding light, and for showing me the beauty of a mother's love. I am truly blessed to have you. I love you, Mama.

My incredible cousin Lou, the journey we've shared in steering life's unpredictable twists and turns have been nothing short of a blessing. From day one, your support has been a guiding light through my darkest moments, and your understanding of my story surpasses that of most. It's truly a testament to the intense connection we share.

Your role as my day one 'ride or die' has been nothing short of remarkable, providing solace and strength during times of adversity. As we've faced life's challenges together, your sisterly guidance has been a source of comfort, offering insights that only someone who truly understands my journey could provide. Your ability to empathise and share in both the joys and sorrows has created a unique connection that goes beyond the limits of just family ties.

I want to express my deepest gratitude for the constant encouragement you've provided. Your belief in me has been a driving force, propelling me forward even when faced with uncertainty. Looking ahead, I am excited about the prospect of continuing our journey of growth and support. With you by my side, I am confident that we can face whatever challenges come our way, and celebrate the triumphs that life has in store for us.

Thank you, Louise, for being more than a cousin – for being a cherished part of my heart on this remarkable journey called life.

To my bestie Julia, my unexpected angel, you came into my life right when I needed you most and I am grateful for you. Your existence has been a source of comfort and solace through the twists and turns of life. Thank you, for providing a safe haven where I can authentically be myself. Your acceptance and understanding have created a space where vulnerability is embraced, and I can shed the masks that life often demands. Opening your arms wide and welcoming me into your family is a testament to the depth of our connection. The warmth, love and craziness (LOL) within your family have become an extension of my own, and I cherish the sense of belonging you've granted me.

Life without you by my side is unimaginable now. You have become more than a friend; you are my sister for life. The bond we share transcends ordinary friendship. Your daily encouragement serves as a lifeline, a reminder of my capabilities, potential, and worth. Even in moments when it appears that I may not be listening, rest assured, your words and support are not lost on me. I internalise them, drawing strength from them when needed most.

Julia, you are undeniably one of my biggest inspirations. Your resilience, kindness, and loving spirit motivate me to be a better person. Our journey together is filled with shared laughter, tears, and growth. Your friendship is a treasure, and I look forward to continuing this remarkable journey with you by my side.

My dear friend Laura, you are more than just a friend; you are the other half of me, my kindred spirit and confidante. Thank you for the invaluable role you've played in my journey of self-discovery. Your presence has been a catalyst for reminding me of my true essence. In moments when I may have lost sight of who I am, you've been there to gently guide me back to my authentic self. Your insight and understanding have been a beacon of clarity, helping me navigate the complexities of who I am.

One of the most beautiful aspects of our friendship is your ability to bring out my inner child. In a world that often demands seriousness, you've created a space where laughter, playfulness, and spontaneity are not only welcomed but celebrated. Your encouragement to embrace the childlike wonder within me has been instrumental in healing the more vulnerable parts of my being.

Thank you, Laura, for allowing me to open up my heart completely during this shared journey. Your genuine acceptance and support have created an environment where vulnerability is not a weakness, but a source of strength. The process of baring my soul, guided by your understanding, has contributed significantly to the emotional and spiritual growth that has shaped me into the warrior I am today.

Your patience during moments when I feel like I'm losing my mind is a testament to the depth of our friendship. Our shared experiences, like climbing trees and grounding ourselves in nature, have become not just activities but therapeutic rituals that allow my soul to heal.

Laura, you are the yin to my yang – a perfect match that brings balance and harmony to our friendship. The love and appreciation I feel for you goes beyond words. Your influence has sculpted me into a stronger, more resilient individual, and I am so grateful for the role you've played in my life.

My Reiki Master, Carole, you have been an instrumental force in my healing process, guiding me through challenges and helping me emerge stronger. Thank you for the crucial role you played in helping me reclaim my voice. In moments when I felt silenced by the weight of my experiences, you provided a safe space for expression and empowerment. Your guidance has been an inspiration, leading me back to a place of self-affirmation and authenticity.

The release of pain and trauma from my life has been an essential aspect of our journey together. Your expertise in Reiki, combined with your empathetic understanding, created the perfect environment for healing.

Carole, your unique ability to balance my chakras has been transformative. This has not only contributed to my emotional well-being but has also had a positive ripple effect on various aspects of my life. Beyond being a guide on my spiritual journey, you have become a wonderful friend. Your compassion, wisdom, and genuine care have enriched our connection beyond just Reiki sessions. The trust and connection we share extend beyond the spiritual realm, creating a foundation for a friendship that I value deeply.

Thank you, Carole, for playing a such a huge role in helping me reclaim my personal power. I express my heartfelt gratitude for your role in my life – as a healer, guide, and most importantly friend. The positive transformations I've experienced are a testament to your expertise. I am truly blessed to have you as a part of my journey.

To all those mentioned in this book, whether still part of my life or not, you have also shaped my journey and played vital roles. Even to my womb donor, this book wouldn't be possible without you.

To my online followers, you provide me with courage daily. You remind me of the strength needed to persevere, and your motivation pushes me forward. This book is for all of you—because, let's be real, we didn't get the mothers we deserved, but we're in this together. Here's hoping I've done our story justice and helped a few of you along the way.

And finally, to my younger self, I am sorry you didn't get the life you deserved, but I will fight every day to ensure I become the person you always needed. No one's got your back quite like I do, and I'm determined to make you proud. This journey is about rewriting our story, and I'm dedicated to ensuring that the future holds the love and happiness you didn't get to experience.

Love to you all, Kylie

CHAPTER 1
FRAGILE FOUNDATIONS

"Mother: *a person who loves unconditionally; the maker of and keeper of memories; a person much loved and greatly admired.*"

This is how most people would describe a Mother. Unfortunately, a lot more people than you realise would have a completely different view on this. Myself included. When I think of my mother, the words that come to mind are: *heartless, evil, narcissistic, abuser, poisonous and unworthy.*

Now, don't get me wrong! I didn't always think these things of my mother, but I'm no longer a naive child. Let's not skip ahead just yet though. First, let me give you the backstory into why I cut my mother off for good…

It was the summer of 1988. I was about four months old and I was wearing a pink velour baby grow while I lay in my baby basket next to my Grandmother. Don't ask me how I remember this day; it has always been one of the earliest memories I have. I didn't know much, but I knew I was happy and I felt safe. My Grandmother was babysitting me. I loved my Grandmother, her face was so warm, she had a cheeky smile and always smelt of moth balls. She was born and raised in Calcutta, India. She had the softest, silk like, olive-coloured skin and her nails were always painted with polish.

As I lay there staring at my Grandmother's face filled with love, she told me all about what she was watching on the television. This part of the memory is a little harder to remember, but I she did say that I was an angel and such a good baby. I've always been ahead of my years, so it doesn't surprise me when I look back on this memory and have such a clear recollection of it.

The rest of my memories before the age of four years old are very hazy. I have hundreds of memories with my cousins. We were very close as kids, something that you don't see very often with this generation. My relationship with my cousins had a Goonies vibe to it. We were always outside doing something; even little me was part of the gang. When I think about my cousins, I can honestly say that they gave me the best childhood memories.

We used to play this game called *'Runaways'* which, in hindsight, was a little ironic to my upbringing. We would pretend our parents were abusive, and we would dress head to toe in black clothes so we could plan our escape once our parents had gone to bed. My cousins would tie a dressing gown robe to the doors and pretend we were zip lining out of the windows by running under them, holding onto a hanger we had connected to the dressing gown rope. The runaways felt so real! I loved them. Perhaps my subconscious wanted them to be real. I used to spend most weekends at my cousin's house, which I am grateful for.

I'm not sure where my mother was, I know she worked in a nightclub when I was quite young, but I'm unsure how old I was when she stopped working there. She could have been with one of her "boyfriends" besides my father (who we will get to in good time). My mother spent a lot of time with a man named Bobby. As a child, you don't understand relationships, but looking back, I know exactly what Bobby was to my mother. I wouldn't say they were an item, but they had their benefits. Occasionally, we would go to Bobby's house. He lived with his mother. I can't remember her name, but I know she had a blonde perm, the complete opposite to Bobby who had taken to his true Italian heritage with his dark hair and tanned skin.

One day, we were at Bobby's- I was quite young as I was in my buggy. I had woken up and was crying. Bobby's mother was shouting to him and at my mother, telling them "shut that child up." I don't know where my mother was but I remember a lot of shouting and the mention of "coke," which in a vague flashback type memory and I can see Bobby doing cocaine. I can't tell you if my mother ever did it with him, but I do remember her smoking marijuana. I used to watch her roll her joint on the bed while I played with my toys, and then she would smoke it whilst watching me play.

When I wasn't with my cousins, or being dragged to god knows where by my mother, I was with my first true love, my Grandmother. My mother and I lived with her for the first few years of my life and I had a very special bond with her. For the first two years of my life, my Aunty Sarah also lived there with my Uncle Stu. I used to sit outside their bedroom door, on my potty, shouting "fatty". Sarah was pregnant with my cousin Brad at the time.

One memory that stays strong was Christmas. It snowed more than I have ever known it to snow. I went outside with Sarah and Stu and we made the biggest snowman ever. I don't remember if my mother was there. I don't know if she simply wasn't around, or if my mind has blocked her out from all of my happy childhood memories.

I loved having a full house! It was like I craved interaction with other people. In a way, I still love a full house. The chaos almost comforts me. When Sarah had Brad, they moved out. Luckily, they only went across the road, so I wasn't too lonely. Brad was more like a brother than a cousin to me. There are exactly 3 years and 3 days between us and we were always together. When my Grandmother looked after us, we always got to sleep in her bed. I can still smell the moth balls she had in her wardrobe. To me this was a smell of comfort and safety. My Grandmother would put Vicks on our chests before bed. I'm still not sure why she used to do this, as we didn't have colds, it was just part of her bedtime ritual.

So, I am yet to mention my Father. Where do I start? He was never really around. My Mother claimed that he never wanted her to have me, as I was the result of an affair and he had a wife and kids in Birmingham. Looking back, I'm not sure how much truth there is to this as there are many pictures of my Father and my cousin Ashton. There are even a few of him and I.

Whatever the truth is, I know he is not someone I want in my life. Up until the age of 3, I recall my father randomly coming over to stay. He came very late, so it wasn't to see me. The clearest memory I have of my Father isn't one that makes me want to start planning for a family reunion. I was crying and he pointed a gun in my face and told me to shut up. Although I was too young to understand the dangers of a gun, I knew the purpose of a gun. One of my favourite movies was "Who Framed Roger Rabbit," so I knew only the bad guys pointed guns at people.

My memories of my father are very sparse, apart from one night when my mother dragged me out of bed to go and see him at his brother's house. It must have been late as there was hardly anyone out and it was freezing. I remember looking around the street, a small child surrounded by the cold, dark sky, darting across roads with my little legs, trying to keep up with my mother who was dragging me behind her. We spent the rest of the night in a room which I can only compare to what looked like a squat. There were beer cans everywhere and the room had a stale smell of cigarettes. My mother and father were smoking marijuana and my father sat there with a beer in his hand, drunk and spilling it all over the place as he spoke to me. I can still smell the stench of beer on his breath; maybe this is why I hate the smell of it so much now. I was young but it was very apparent that my father had a habit of being drunk. I don't know where he disappeared to after this, but it wasn't the last time I saw him.

CHAPTER 2
MY FOREVER ANGEL

When I was four years old, my Aunty Angela became very ill. She had cancer. I didn't understand what this meant, but I knew it was bad. I idolised my Aunty Angela. There was something so fascinating about her soul - she was the definition of warm and fuzzy. She had the most beautiful long, dark curly hair. She looked like a mermaid. She used to travel a lot, mainly to the Caribbean with her boyfriend, John and they always brought me back presents.

Angela's health was deteriorating. One day, she came over wearing a headscarf. As she sat and spoke with my mother and my other aunties, she removed the scarf. Her once beautiful mermaid hair was now a thing of the past as she showed off her completely bald head. She started shouting at the dog to stop staring at her; she was feeling insecure about her appearance. Something had changed in her, that warm, fuzzy feeling was gone. I felt a sadness so deep, it made my stomach hurt.

Shortly after, Angela came to live at my Grandmother's house with us. My mother and John were Angela's main carers while she was ill. She couldn't manage the stairs so she slept on the sofa all day, every day. I used to sit with her chatting away, although, most of the time, she fell asleep. I watched her, wondering why all of her hair had gone; her face had become extremely thin and her eyes sunk into her head. I questioned why she looked so sad. I hardly ever left her side.

She also couldn't make it to the toilet so she had a commode. I didn't understand what the commode was until Angela started shouting at everyone and refusing to use it. She wanted to go to the bathroom I remember saying to her "Just use your potty, Aunty! I used to have one too, it's ok."

At school, I pretended everything was ok. That was when I began to learn the meaning of putting on a brave face. Yet, I was still a nervous little girl at the same time. Angela has always encouraged me to use my voice. She always had my back if my mother was telling me off about something. Even from as young as four, I didn't feel like I could speak up around my mother.

There was a dinner lady at my school who had the same scary demeanour that my mother had. One day, I needed to go to the toilet at the end of lunch, but when I asked the dinner lady she wouldn't let me go. I knew not to speak up, so I didn't argue with her. I soiled myself that day, but was too scared to tell anyone. I went through the rest of the day in my soiled pants, and then disposed of them when I got home because I was too scared to tell my mother in fear of getting in trouble.

I became more and more of a recluse. Everyone was busy caring for Angela, but I just wanted her to get up and be that hero she had always been. One day, as I was colouring pictures next to her, my mother came in. She told me to tell Angela that I loved her and to go upstairs and make her a picture. So I did just that. As I sat in my room drawing away, I heard Angela saying "Aunty La La La needs to go away now, but I will always be close by." I wasn't at all concerned that she wasn't actually there in the room. Her spirit was there with me, reassuring me, saying goodbye. I could even smell her. I will never forget the smell of her White Musk perfume.

Shortly after, my mother came up to tell me that Angela had died. I told her that I knew and told her what had just happened. My mother didn't quite know how to take it, but I always knew and still know that my Aunty is here, always close by, watching over me like my guardian angel. And whenever I am at my lowest, without a fail, I will smell that White Musk.

Angela's death was hard! Even though I was so young, I was aware of what had happened. I loved my Aunty so much. She was my best friend and I have so many wonderful memories with her, despite only having such a short time together. Even now, as I write this, I have tears flooding down my face. Over thirty years since she passed, her memory still lives strong in my heart. As I have grown older and heard stories about the kind of person she was, I have found comfort in realising that I am very similar to her: a stubborn free spirit. And I know she is still fighting my corner and I've made her proud.

Soon after Angela died, my mother and I moved into her flat. It was a tower block in West London. My mother and aunties cleared Angela's things as I sat and tried on her jewellery; she had a lot! Every single one of Angela's fingers was always covered in gold rings and she would wear 3 or 4 gold chains at a time. I came across a load of 'Sad Sam' teddies; they were these sad looking dogs with big puffy heads. The look on their faces reminded me of Angela's face when she was sad; I decided that I would keep them so that I could always remember her.

I'm not sure how long we stayed at Angela's flat, but with it being council property we weren't allowed to stay long. One day, someone knocked at the door. My mother told me to be quiet and we both waited for whoever was at the door to leave. We used to do this a lot and it became normal to me to be quiet anytime anyone knocked at the door. After about 20 minutes of knocking, I heard drilling at the door. I was so scared, thinking that there was a bad man outside trying to get in. My mother was frantic at the time, unsure of what to do. She opened the door, only to realise that they were boarding over the door as we weren't supposed to be there. They gave us a few days to collect our things. We left to go back to my Grandmother's. When we moved back, there were a lot of arguments; my Grandmother and my mother always clashed and everything caused a fight.

CHAPTER 3
SOMETHING DOESN'T FEEL RIGHT…

When I was five, we moved out of my Grandmother's to a flat 3 miles away. It was a two bedroom with a huge living room. I loved having so much space! I used to ride my tricycle round and round in circles in the living room. I had my own room and my Granddad painted it pink for me. I had a great relationship with my Granddad too. I often sat and watched him when he was decorating. It was fascinating to see him dressed casually. Every other day he was wearing a suit and tie, with what was left of his grey hair slicked back. He kept a comb in the top pocket of his suit jacket, so he was always sure to be well-polished.

My Granddad was Polish and had a very fair complexion in comparison to my Grandmother. My mother got more of her father's genes - her skin was so pale, she was almost translucent. It didn't help that she had the darkest, polka straight hair; it made her look even more washed out. She didn't get my grandparents' warm natures however. She had a hard face; her eyes were always sunken and she never smiled. Yet, despite her cold exterior, there was something I still loved about my mother. I mean, she was my mother, right? I had my own room but I still shared a room with my mother. I slept in her bed and used my room as a playroom.

We had a lot of fun during those times. We rented movies and had cinema days where we closed all the curtains, put the sofa right in front of the TV and ate loads of popcorn. These are some of the few happy memories I do have with my mother.

I don't have much recollection of school during this time. I had to start at a new school when we moved. We moved in June and the school year started in September, although I didn't start straight away. I remember going into a new class where everyone else had already started. I'm not sure why my attendance was so bad, but I missed a lot of school. I managed to make a nice group of friends, but due to my attendance I was required to go out for extra support with the kids we used to refer to as "the smelly ones". I was always very tired at school, sometimes too tired to function, and I often used to be told off for sleeping at my desk.

I did like living in our new flat, but I sometimes missed the company. Brad still used to stay over a lot, but I started to dislike my mother's favouritism towards him. Brad could do no wrong. One morning, I woke up covered in urine after Brad and I had slept in my mother's bed. Confused and feeling cold, I went to find my mother and ask her why I was wet. Her and Brad were watching the snow out of the window.

She turned to me and said, "Yes, Brad wet the bed and it went all over you, just go and clean yourself up."

I stood there for a moment, thinking, *She let me lie in his wee?!*

I always felt like Brad was the son my mother had always wanted. She was different towards him, like she actually loved him. She showed him affection and I think this was part of the reason why I started to dislike him. Why was he getting all the hugs? Why was she telling him that she loved him? I can count on one hand the amount of times my mother has hugged me in my entire life, and even those times it felt weird. I honestly do not think my mother loved me; she certainly never told me she did.

Soon after the move, my mother met Mike, who worked in our local newsagents. He was 20 years old when they met, 6 years younger than my mother. His parents owned the shop and he used to run it for them. We used to go in there after school, and one day, he asked my mother her name and she introduced us both to him. I thought he said his name was Mince, so I called him that for a while. He was very chatty. We started to go into the shop a lot after that day and we'd spend ages in there. I used to sit on the shelf and read all the magazines while he and my mother were talking.

After a few weeks, Mike started coming round to our house in the evenings, and eventually my mother told me that he was her boyfriend. I was so upset! I told my mother I didn't like him, probably because she was spending no time with me and all her time with him. Since she started dating him, I spent more time at my Grandmother's or my Aunty Katrina's house while she went out. I felt left out. She explained to him that it wasn't going to work as I wasn't happy. Obviously, Mike wasn't going to just accept this, so he devoted three weeks to giving me non-stop attention. I would go on date night with them to the arcade and Mike would win me loads of prizes from the claw grabbing games. I would lie in the back of his delivery van playing with all of my new toys on the drive back home. Looking back now, this wasn't the safest form of transporting a five year old, but I guess things were a lot more lenient back in the 90s. Mike continued to shower me with presents, and just like any five year old, I came around and started to like him. Then he and my mother became official.

I started to feel more and more like an inconvenience. Gone were the cinema sofa days and I had to spend more and more time alone. I felt like a prisoner in my room all day every day. Why were the weekends so long? Why did the school holidays last so long? I longed to be at school. I would line all my teddies up and pretend they were my students while I taught them their daily lessons. I felt lonely, like I didn't have anyone to talk to.

Mike's parents didn't approve of his relationship with my mother. There was one evening when I was sitting in the shop on the shelf reading magazines, when Mike's father came in and literally threw us out, screaming and shouting at my mother calling her a "white slag". It was never easy after this. We would be at my Aunty's house for Christmas, playing games and eating food, then Mike's father would ring and because he knew that Mike was with my mother, he would say "you need to come home now or I am locking the doors." So my traditional Christmas with my family, the highlight of every Christmas for me, was cut short because Mike had to leave.

I hated how much my mother put him before me. Maybe it was jealousy, as it had just being the two of us for so long, or maybe it was my survival instinct from having to fight harder for her attention. I used to wish so hard for him to disappear; to just leave like my father had. My mother had a cork board that was covered in photographs of the two of them. I used to take the pins and stick them in his eyes on every single photo.

Mike wasn't always bad in my eyes. One time, I was sat playing school with my teddies and the buzzer went. My mother actually answered it on this occasion; she usually liked to pretend we weren't home anytime someone came to the door. It was my father. I could hear him drunk, shouting down the intercom that he wanted to see me. I begged my mother not to let him in. Somehow, he managed to get into the building and was banging at the front door shouting, "Open the door! Let me in!" He started kicking the door. I was petrified. Did he have his gun? Was he going to kill me?

My mother rang Mike. He came to our place and told my father he had to leave. There was a lot of abusive language from my father, but eventually he left. I looked out the window to make sure I saw him leave. He looked in a state, and as he stumbled over and lay on the gutter, I prayed he would never come back. That was the last time I saw him.

The whole ordeal terrified me. Mike had come to the rescue but as I sat in my room going over this traumatic event, no one came to ask me if I was okay. My mother sat with Mike and I went back to hating him. I needed my mother to come and comfort me at that point. I sat there crying alone, hoping my father wouldn't come back.

A few days later, my father's friend, Franklin, came around to say that my father had gone back to Birmingham. Franklin had a lot of time for me and I really liked him. He was always playing games with me and he started to spend a lot more time at our house. He would look after me while my mother was out with Mike and he would sleepover on the sofa a lot. My mother and Franklin grew closer and eventually they would have "sleepovers" in my mother's bed. As a child, all this seemed innocent to me. It's crazy what you realise when you begin to look back on things as an adult.

My mother seemed happy when Franklin was around. She would twist his hair into locks for him and clean his ears with cotton buds. They also smoked a lot of marijuana. They used to leave it lying around; I picked it up and smelled it whenever I saw it. There was something about the smell that I found comfort in, perhaps I associated the smell with times my mother was actually happy. My cat got hold of their marijuana once and ate it; he couldn't walk in a straight line for days.

Franklin took me to school sometimes too. We had to go the long way, so that we didn't go past Mike's shop. Franklin said that if Mike saw him, he would be upset.

By now, I was about half way through Year 2 in school. I was nearly seven years old. I was struggling with my story writing as I had missed a lot of school. My teacher said I needed to practise my writing at home. My mother never sat with me to help with schoolwork; she was always too busy. On this particular day she was sorting out my old baby clothes.

I started to help her when she said, "Do you want to know why I am sorting these clothes out?" I looked at her confused, while she excitedly shouted "I'm having a baby."

CHAPTER 4
A BUNDLE OF JOY OR AN EIGHT YEAR OLD'S BURDEN

I burst into tears and begged her to tell me she was joking. I didn't want a brother or a sister. It was already hard enough for me to get any attention from her; I didn't want to share her with anyone else. Most of my mother's pregnancy was a blur. Mike was still on curfew with his parents so wasn't around much. Franklin was around some of the time, but he never mentioned the drama we had with my father, even though he gave me a birthday card from him for my 7th birthday. When I opened the card and saw it said "Happy 5th Birthday", I gave it back to him and told him I didn't want it.

The night my mother went into labour, I was at a friend's house. Mike and my Aunty Sarah came to pick me up and took me to my Aunty Katrina's house. I barely slept that night. I was just thinking that I was about to become a big sister. I didn't know how I felt about it and I was still very unsure about the whole situation. What was a big sister meant to do? What if I wasn't good at it? Would my mother be mad at me? In the morning, my Granddad came to pick me up and take me home. By then, I was more excited about the idea of becoming a sister. I made a card for my new baby sister and I waited at the window for them to come home.

My sister Kiara arrived. I will never forget the day I first met her! She was so tiny, she smelt so new and fresh. *So this was the baby smell people went on about.* She had a red baby-grow on when I met her for the first time. I helped my mother bathe her in her little baby bath. The smell of Johnson's baby still reminds me of that day. I wanted to smell just like her, so I squeezed into her bath after she was finished. Maybe having a baby sister wouldn't be so bad; at least I would have someone to talk to now.

Mike couldn't admit to his parents that he was with my mother, so he wasn't around much, just a few hours in the evening when Kiara was already asleep. My mother and I were walking past Mike's shop one day with Kiara in the buggy, when we saw Mike's mother and she asked who the baby was. My mother responded:

"Oh, I'm a child-minder now. She's one of the babies I look after."

Why was she lying? I thought to myself. I so badly wanted to call her out on her blatant lie, but I knew what was good for me so I kept my mouth shut. Even as an eight year old I knew this was disgraceful, having to hide your own daughter.

I helped my mother a lot with Kiara, since Mike wasn't around. Sometimes she left me alone with her while she popped to the shops. Kiara would lie there asleep, on the bed, and I would have to sit and watch her until my mother came back. I sat there thinking about how much I didn't like her, as since she came along I had to act as a parent rather than a sister. Perfecting how to change a nappy at the age of eight wasn't something to class as an achievement. All I wanted to do was play with my Barbies.

When Kiara was about 4-5 months old, Franklin came over with his girlfriend. I don't remember much about the visit, but I do remember my mother kicking off after Franklin's girlfriend asked, "Is she Franklin's then?"

My mother started shouting. "So you only brought her here to check if she was yours? Well, look at her! Does she look like she's yours?" Then she kicked them both out and that was the last we ever saw of Franklin. Looking back on this as an adult, I suddenly realised the true meaning of their "sleepovers" and having to go the long way around to school. He could have been my sister's father.

Of course my mother never mentioned the Franklin incident to Mike and it wasn't long after that my mother called me out of bed. She and Mike were in her room with Kiara and my mother said she had something to tell me.

"You are going to have another brother or sister."

The words ripped through me. Everything went quiet and I was screaming inside. I cried and cried, more than I had when she told me about Kiara. I told her I didn't even want the sister I had, let alone another one. Mike barely pulled his weight with the one baby. His parents still didn't know about Kiara and there was another one on the way; another baby that I would have to help my mother take care of, another baby that would take away any hope I had left of being a child. I hated everyone.

I went to bed and did what was starting to become a regular occurrence for me: I closed my eyes and imagined a different life. I imagined I was a princess, living in a big castle, having big, grand balls every day, surrounded by love and happiness. Little did I know, I was trying to escape my reality, every, single, day. Eight years old and I already knew this life wasn't for me. I imagined I had another mother too, one that loved me and showered me with affection… In my dreams, eh?

Needless to say, this pregnancy was also a blur. Towards the end of her pregnancy, I caught chicken pox and passed it to Kiara. I was off school, but due to my extremely poor attendance my sister's health visitor came to check up on me. There I was, asleep in my bed and I was woken up by this woman, who reminded me of the Wicked Witch of the East from The Wizard of Oz, checking my body to make sure I did have chicken pox, inspecting me from head to toe, while I stood there half asleep. When she was happy that it was indeed chicken pox, I was allowed to get back into bed.

After we'd recovered from the chicken pox, my mother had the baby, and just like that I had a brother, Kevin. I don't remember my first meeting with Kevin as well as I do Kiara's. My Grandmother was looking after me, Kiara, Brad and his younger sister Lucy, while my mother was at the hospital. Brad had burst my beanbag all over the place and as soon as my mother got home, she started shouting at everyone began was hoovering all the beans up, so this memory overrides the memory of meeting my brother Kevin.

There are thirteen months between Kiara and Kevin. Mike still hadn't moved in because of his parents. So, now at the age of eight, soon to be nine, I was a pro at looking after two babies. I was late for school every day, on the days I went to school, that is. I remember the routine like it was yesterday; I had done it that many times.

My mother would wake us up. I would give the babies their bottles while my mother went to wash her hair. I would then have to change both babies' nappies and get them dressed, while sitting through the torture of Milkshake, a morning programme on Channel 5 that played baby programmes. By the time all of this was done, my mother would be ready and I would then go off to have my breakfast and get myself ready for school.

I loved going to school at this time. It was a break away from being the babysitter and I actually got to be a child for a while. My mother still had me off school a lot of the time. One afternoon, there was a phone call from her at school. The teacher took me to the phone and my mother said that she had told them I might have head lice, because she needed to come and get me early. It was a complete lie and I didn't want to leave, but she came and got me. She probably wanted to have her afternoon nap and couldn't settle her children.

As well as my morning routines with the babies, I also had to watch them when I got home from school. Kiara was a handful and I disliked her because she was so naughty, she would do something wrong and I would be the one to get in trouble. After dinner, it was bath time. I would bathe the babies, then after my mother would get into their bath and top it up as she liked to have a soak. Whilst she relaxed, I would get them both dried, creamed and dressed, and then read them their bedtime story. After all of this, I was exhausted.

CHAPTER 5
UNEDUCATED, ME?

All of this responsibility meant that I was rarely at school. My attendance was so poor I'd missed a big chunk of Year 3 and 4 especially. My attendance had never been great, but these school years had a big effect on me. I missed out on learning about the Tudors, the Romans, and a huge chunk of Geography. Still, to this day, I haven't been able to get a grasp of these areas. The school was concerned about my attendance and one day, when I turned up at school, there were some social workers there to talk to me. I struggle to remember exactly what happened, but I knew they were going to be there as my mother had pre-warned me. She also told me that they wanted to take me away, so I had to tell them I was ill with my stomach aches. I started to panic. She had told me that if they took me away, I would live with another family who wouldn't be nice to me and would do horrible things to me.

The social workers were asking me why I was off school so much, if I was ill, if my mother spoke about my Aunty Angela much. From what I could work out, my mother had told them she was still struggling with Angela's death and keeping me with her comforted her. I cried and told them I wanted my mother.

When I finished school that day, my mother was eagerly waiting to find out how the meeting went. She was actually on time to pick me up, for once. She was usually at least 15 minutes late. I told her what happened and of course she kicked off. She rang the school and started screaming down the phone that they had scared me so much I was too worried to come back to school. I didn't feel this way at all. I was just confused. Why did social services want to take me away? Why was I having so much time off school? Something felt wrong. I felt like I was missing something, but I didn't quite know what it was.

There was not long left of Year 4 when I did return. The head teacher, Mrs Seville, was leaving for a new school and had set a competition for all students to draw a self-portrait, as she would then choose three of her favourites to hang up in her new office. I really wanted to win! Mrs Seville had invested a lot of time in me over the years, trying to improve my attendance, and I wanted my picture to go up in her office so she would never forget me.

That afternoon, when I got home from school, I got my best drawing paper and laid out all my felt tips on the floor. I started sketching away, determined to make it my best drawing ever to ensure that I would be chosen as a winner. My mother walked past my room and saw me lying on my floor colouring away, when she asked me what I was doing. I told her all about the competition and how much I wanted to win. I explained to her why I thought I had a good chance. I'm not sure what I was expecting from this encounter with my mother, as she was never one to offer words of encouragement. I was not prepared to be as disappointed as I was when she looked at it in disgust.

"I don't know why you are wasting your time; you're never going to win. That doesn't even look like you!"

I was devastated by her response, but it just made me more determined to do well and prove her wrong. I handed in my picture the next day and we had to wait a whole week before we found out who the winners were. I saw a lot of my friends' pictures; they were really good and actually looked like them. I started to think my mother was right. There was no way I was going to win with the standard of the other portraits. My friends were all so talented and so creative. I didn't even compare when I was up against them. I started to wonder what my talents were and where they could take me in the future. I wasn't good at English or Maths, I couldn't draw or sing, I wasn't even very athletic. The only thing I was really good at was looking after babies. I had definitely perfected that one.

We had a whole school assembly on the last day of school so that Mrs Seville could say her goodbyes and announce the winners of the competition. The suspense of the competition was killing me, having to sit through all the songs, assembly awards and Year 6 graduations. I just wanted to find out who had won. There were over 400 children in that school and there were only three winners. Due to the amount of portraits to choose from though, Mrs Seville decided to have three runners up as well. They only won a head teacher award, but it was still worth it.

As she called the three runners up, I waited on edge to see if my name would be called. I hadn't been chosen. There was no way I was winning anything now. My mother was right. My picture was rubbish. I was so saddened that I had drifted off into a world of my own, when suddenly my friend was nudging me, "you won," she said. I looked at her confused. I won? I looked at Mrs Seville and she was holding up my portrait. I had won 1st prize. Out of all these children, she chose me. I was ecstatic! I had never won anything in my life and, more importantly, I had proved my mother wrong. From that day forward, I promised myself I would never let anyone tell me I couldn't. If I wanted to do something then I would do it, no matter what anyone said.

CHAPTER 6
STANDSTILL SUMMERS

School was out for summer, which meant six long weeks of being at home with the kids. I don't have many memories about what I did in my summer holidays, as we never went away and we didn't really do much. The odd trip to the seaside to see my Grandmother was the best we got. She had moved there just before Kiara was born, so I didn't get to see her as often as I used to. These visits were usually cut short because my mother would just end up arguing with my Grandmother and we would come home after two days.

That was about as exciting as my summer holidays got. We used to go shopping a lot, mainly to Hounslow, which was about a ten minute drive from where we lived. With two young children, these trips required two buggies, which meant that I had to push one of these around while Mike would push the other. My mother rarely pushed a buggy herself. I hated these shopping trips! They consisted of me sitting at the front of the shop with the buggies, waiting for my mother because it was too crowded to push them around.

By September, I couldn't wait to get back to school and see my friends. I never got to meet up with them during the summer; most of them were away on holiday. The ones that did stay, I wasn't allowed to hang out with. One time, I had arranged a playdate with my friend Zara, after my mother and I had bumped into her and her mother on the way back from the shops.

Zara's mother said she would come and collect me the next day so I could go and play at their house for a few hours. I was so excited, I woke up super early - counting down the hours until they arrived. When they did finally arrive, my mother made me sit in silence while they knocked at the door, pretending that we weren't home. They knocked for ten minutes before they left.

One thing I hated about going back to school was that everyone talked about their summer holidays, then would ask "so what did you do?" I never had anything exciting to talk about.

I was starting Year 5 at school. Things were getting really serious. The work was getting a lot harder in preparation for secondary school. I did struggle to adapt to the amount of work required for this year. Missing out on so much school in the previous years meant that I wasn't fully prepared for this. I found it hard to concentrate because I was already tired from the work I had to do at home.

I had quite a substantial amount of time off during that year. Apparently, I had issues with going to the toilet and I would get really ill if I couldn't go; slightly exaggerated in hindsight. I remember this being a problem, yet I don't remember it being often enough to account for numerous days off from school.

There was a time where I had to go to the hospital and have tons of tests. I even had to have a scan. I remember looking at the screen thinking I would see a baby, as this was the only thing I associated with scans. I was prodded and poked, appointment after appointment.

I kept getting urine infections. As an adult, I now know that I get one whenever I'm not drinking enough water throughout the day. My mother took me to the doctors and I was told to go and lie on the bed behind the curtain and take my knickers off. I remember feeling really awkward as I did, something didn't feel right. My male doctor then examined my genital area. I had never felt so uncomfortable in my life. I lay there stiff as he prodded and poked down there before saying I would need to be referred for further tests. I didn't know and still don't really know what had happened, but I never wanted to see that doctor again, and I never did.

Shortly after, the appointments for my stomach problems just stopped. The doctors said they couldn't find anything wrong with me and that was that, it was never spoken of again and I didn't seem to have a problem anymore. It's odd because I truly believed there was a problem, but was this because it had been drummed into me that there was a problem?

Back at school, my classmates were deciding on what to do for the class assembly. We decided to go with the story 'The Tortoise and the Hare'. Our teacher asked for a show of hands for people to take each role. I really wanted to be the hare, but my teacher said she couldn't give me the lead role because of my attendance. I was so upset.

After school, I told my mother about the assembly and how I had been chosen to be a tree because I wasn't allowed to be the hare. She didn't even let me finish before she marched over to my teacher. I ran after her, trying to make her stop and listen to why I wasn't allowed to be the hare, but it was too late. She started shouting at my teacher, asking why I wasn't allowed to have the part. When she eventually stopped ranting and allowed my teacher to get a word in, she was told that this was due to my poor attendance. My mother turned to me and, in front of my teacher, said:

"You never told me that bit. You just made me look an idiot. I'm not coming to your assembly to watch you be a tree."

She walked off and left me standing there. I was so embarrassed, I wanted the ground to swallow me up. I looked at my teacher and she looked really sorry for me. I think she could see the sadness in my eyes from the way my mother had just reacted. She put her hand on my shoulder and was just about to say something when my mother appeared and screamed at me to come with her. I ran off and walked home in silence.

The whole way home I was extremely nervous. I was getting the silent treatment, which was my mother's favourite punishment. I hated it. Not knowing what was on her mind and what could happen next was the most terrifying experience I have ever lived through. Unless you have been subject to excessive silent treatment, you won't understand the feeling of loneliness, isolation and despair it can cause.

I would try to make small talk with her to gauge where her head was at, and the more she ignored me, the tighter the knots in my stomach got. She had never acted this way in front of anyone else before. *What if those people from social services came to take me away?* I felt so alone, it was unreal! Ten years old and I was so confused about the world. Surely, this isn't what life is meant to be like! It wasn't like this in the movies. I guess happy ever afters are just fairy tales, a make-believe world where everything is unicorns and flowers.

The next day at school, my teacher called me over. She said she had thought about the assembly and was giving me a chance to be the hare, but that my attendance needed to be one hundred percent up until the assembly, or she would give it to someone else. She got me to promise that I would learn all my lines and that I would let her know if I was struggling. I was so excited! I promised I would not let her down, and off I went to learn my lines. Nobody had ever given me a chance to prove myself. I was not going to let my teacher down; she was the first person to ever believe in me.

When I told my mother that I had got the lead part in the assembly, she said my teacher had only done it because she was scared of her and that she wouldn't be coming to the assembly anyway. At this point, I didn't care if she was coming or not. My teacher had faith in me, something my mother clearly didn't. I was not going to mess this up. So, my assembly came and it was a great success. My mother wasn't there, but I still felt extremely proud of myself.

I was starting to realise that my mother was extremely hot-headed and stubborn after the incident with my teacher. I had always known that she was like this; I just hadn't really taken much notice of how bad it was. I was very selective with what I told her. She was like a ticking time bomb and you had to approach her with caution: the smallest thing could set her off. She was a funny character, never loving or affectionate. To the world she looked like mother of the year, but behind closed doors she was a cold, heartless witch. And I was beginning to grow a strong dislike towards her.

Things at home had gotten slightly easier for me though. Mike had moved in so at least I wasn't relied on as much, while they played happy families. I always felt like the black sheep, it was like it was them and me. I was the spare piece to the puzzle that didn't fit in.

Mike never treated me like his own. I would sit back and watch Christmas' and Birthdays and the things he would do for his children and compare how different it was when it came to me. Whenever we went to any of his family events, I was always introduced as my mother's daughter. Every Christmas when he would take my siblings to his parents' house; once they actually knew about them, that is. I was left at home with my mother waiting for them to come back. I wasn't his child, so why would he take me?

Mike and my mother weren't the easiest people to grow up with. The arguments were like a norm to me. Even my cousins Brad and Lucy would refer to them as the ones that just fight all the time. The hatred between them was quite apparent, and since moving in with us Mike had become this very bad-tempered man.

We had this one neighbour called Jake, who was a complete waste of space. He used to get drunk and play really loud music. Mike and my mother were constantly having disagreements with him. One day, Jake and Mike got into this massive argument and Mike got the police involved. He made our lives hell after that. Jake would rip our rubbish bags up outside our door, break windows on our car and even shout abuse at me. I was so scared from all the arguments that I couldn't sleep.

It got even worse when we had scaffolding put up on our flat. I was so paranoid from everything that was happening, I thought that Jake would climb the scaffolding and come and kill us. My mother took me to the doctors and they referred me for counselling. I wasn't sure this was what I needed. I think all I wanted was for all these arguments to stop. My mother would put her ear to the wall to hear what Jake was saying about us which would set her off and there would be another bust up. This is how she found out that it was Jake that had smashed our car.

When I started counselling I was so unengaged, I hated going to my sessions. Firstly, they were always during school time and I missed enough of that as it was, and secondly, they never actually spoke about Jake. I snapped and walked out the day she asked me about my father. I felt like it was a complete waste of time, all I wanted was for the arguments to stop and to be back at school with my friends. My father had been out of my life for five years now and had no relevance to anything.

So that was the end of counselling. My mother never took me back after that. The arguments eventually came to an end and I set out to enjoy my final year of primary school. I must admit my attendance in Year 6 was probably the best yet. I learnt a lot and I began to develop a passion for History. I loved learning about the way people used to live and comparing things to life today. I became fascinated by World War One and I really pushed myself to get the most out of my year.

CHAPTER 7
A PRICE TO PAY FOR MY MOTHER'S LIES

I started to find Maths and English a bit easier as well, due to the two classes being split by ability so lessons were more adapted to our own levels rather than trying to teach different abilities at the same time. Mr Sale, the other Year 6 teacher, used to teach me Maths. Not many of the kids in my class liked him as he was quite stern.

One day when we were lining up to leave school for the day, I realised I had forgotten my lunch box, so I quickly jumped out of line to get it. Mr Sale saw me leave the line and grabbed my arm and pulled me to the front. I was only a small skinny girl so it really hurt me.

When I came out of school, my mother noticed me rubbing my arm and asked me what was wrong. I told her what had happened and just like clockwork that ticking time bomb exploded, which is completely normal to any parent. What wasn't normal was her solution to this. We walked the whole way home in silence; me not knowing if she was mad at me. When we got home she picked up the phone screaming and shouting, and made an appointment for the next afternoon to see the head teacher about the incident. I was relieved to realise that it wasn't me she was angry at, maybe she was finally acting like a normal mother because in that moment I felt protected. She actually had my back for a valid reason.

My arm was sore but there was no mark. My mother had plans for this; she said that we needed to make it bruise so that we could get Mr Sale in trouble. That sense of protection I had just been feeling quickly dissipated as she started to pull at my arm in the same place Mr Sale had grabbed me. I started crying from the pain she was causing. There was still no mark though so my mother tied a tea towel round my arm and pulled it really tight. I fought with her to try and make her stop as I was screaming in agony. She held me down while Mike continued to pull at the tea towel. I was begging them to stop, but they didn't. Eventually a mark started to show up. You could see the outline of a hand from where my mother had been pulling at my arm. She was happy with this and marched me down to the police station to report it. The police took photos of my arm and I had to give a statement about what happened with Mr Sale. Obviously, I didn't mention how the mark actually got there. I knew better than that.

The next day, after also recording the incident with my doctor, we went to meet with the head teacher. Mr Sale was there as well, being extremely nice for once. I felt bad and worried he would be arrested for something that had been extremely exaggerated. Mr Sale and the head teacher apologised to my mother over and over, ensuring her this would never happen again and that Mr Sale would be receiving a warning. My mother ranted on and on, just wanting Mr Sale to admit he had grabbed me. After an hour of going back and forth about the situation, my mother said "All I want to know is did you or did you not grab my daughter?" When Mr Sale finally said yes, she replied "Thank you, that's all I wanted to know" and we left.

I am still confused as to what my mother actually wanted to achieve. She so badly needed to hear that he had grabbed me and then she was happy. Was this to make herself feel better for the abuse she had put me through? Maybe she had lied about the story so much she actually believed he was the one to give me those bruises and needed to hear him say he had grabbed me to make it feel true. I just didn't understand how she suddenly forgot about something that had made her so angry.

Well, whatever the motive of that day was, I will never know, but I do know that from that day forward Mr Sale gave me special treatment and constantly walked on eggshells around me. I hated that this was all as a result of a lie.

CHAPTER 8
PUPPETEERING TACTICS

In the true form of my mother, she loved to put the caring parent act on in front of others by kicking up a fuss, but at home she showed little interest. She was always too busy to spend time doing things with me. I had loads of board games, but no one to play them with. I detested my sister more than ever at this time. She was a little madam; she was only two but always arguing with me. I know that as the older sister I should have ignored her, but my mother egged her on. She made my sister refer to me as "Cow-Bitch" and laughed about it. So, naturally my sister thought it was a good thing and would just walk around shouting "Cow-Bitch" at me all day. This used to wind me up so much but if I said anything I would get in trouble.

I used to write about how much I hated them all in my diary, and how my mother never had time to play with me. One day, my mother found my diary and read it. She then confronted me about what I had written. She came in holding my diary shouting, "I never have time for you? No? I never play with you? No? Oh, I'm sorry I'm such a bad mother."

I was so annoyed that she had read my diary, but even more annoyed that she got angry at me for what I had written. Why couldn't she have taken it as an eye opener to want to do more with me rather than give me the silent treatment for the next couple of hours? I became even more isolated. I used to be such a happy, outgoing young girl, but I was becoming a quiet, aloof child who hated her family.

I even started to hate my cousins. One day, Brad came round to stay; as we got older, we fought all the time. During one of our fights he pushed me so hard that I fell into the wardrobe and hurt my back on my roller skates. My eyes filled with tears from the pain and as I sat there and watched Brad and my mother laughing at me, I saw red. I picked up the roller skate and threw it at Brad with all the force I could. He instantly fell to the floor in pain and my mother went crazy. She came running over to me and she hit me. She picked a hanger out of the wardrobe and beat me with it. I ran to my bunk beds and climbed to the top where I knew she wouldn't be able to get to me. She laughed and said, "Oh, you think you're smart, do you?" She sent Brad up to the top bunk to beat me with the hanger and they both started to make a joke of it. I was crying my eyes out in pain and my mother mocked me, asking, "How's it hanging?" Brad and my mother continued to laugh at their new joke and I went to bed. Still to this day, Brad sometimes laughs and asks me, "How's it hanging?"

When it was time to leave primary school, I was quite excited! Just one more summer holiday and I would have so much independence. I had decided to go to a school almost 7 miles away from home. It was also very close to my Aunty Katrina's house, so I knew I would be able to spend a lot of time there. To get ready for secondary school, I enrolled in summer school. I loved the freedom, I travelled so far away from home on my journey to school; it almost felt like I was going on holiday. My Granddad was very ill at this time, he had lung cancer and was in the hospital. Things at home were quite tense, so summer school allowed me to escape all of this.

A week into summer school, I was doing some homework when my mother got a call from my Aunt Katrina. She burst into tears, I instantly knew what this meant - my Granddad had passed away. I was heartbroken. My Granddad was the greatest man I had ever known and many that knew him will tell you the same. He did so much for me, and I loved him dearly. I was eleven when he died and I will never forget the way he only ever wore suits and always carried a comb in his pocket to keep his hair slick. His funeral was hard for me; it was the first one I had been to. I cried my eyes out the whole way through, that by the end, I could barely breathe. The amount of people I had consoling me that day was unreal; the one person that didn't though, was my mother.

CHAPTER 9
THE TEENAGE YEARS

I started secondary school a few weeks later. I was very excited about this new phase of my life. No more having to deal with two children in the mornings. I didn't have to worry about anyone but myself. It took me a while to settle into a school routine, as each term felt longer than ever before. I had a good group of friends to start with, but I soon realised that secondary school girls were much bitchier than primary school girls. One minute, people would be my best friend, the next minute they were my worst enemies. Naturally, I would go home in tears sometimes, and my mother would forbid me from being friends with these girls. Most of the time, I would lie to her and tell her I wasn't friends with them just to keep her off my back.

There was one incident where some girls were being quite malicious. My mother didn't let me go to school and rang the headteacher, saying I wasn't going to be coming back until they sorted it out; quite normal behaviour for a parent really. However, what wasn't normal was the extreme she went to with the girls. She was so angry that she rang them up and left a threatening voicemail calling them "little slags." It was so embarrassing for me to have to go back after. I had made good friends with a girl in a different form group, so it was agreed with the school that I would move to this form group and things were a lot easier from then on.

My mother was still overly protective. I would have to come straight home from school and I was never allowed to stay out. I became friendly with my neighbour, Madeline. She was the same age as me; there were just a few weeks between us. This friendship was dictated by my mother though, she liked to give her opinion on people and sway me towards becoming an unforgiving person. It didn't really feel like I had a mother-daughter relationship with her; she was more like a jealous friend, trying to turn me against the friends I formed bonds with.

During my second year of secondary school, my mother agreed that I could stay at my Aunty Katrina's house during the week, so that I didn't have to travel so far. This was one of the best ideas she ever had. I would go to Katrina's house on a Sunday evening and wouldn't go home until Friday after school. I loved this newfound freedom. There was no requirement for me to come straight home from school, I was allowed to hang out with my friends and, most importantly, I was allowed to come home and just be a kid; no chores, no shouting, just computer games and TV.

It was like I had been checked into a five star hotel. It was also a chance for me to become more independent and prove to my mother I could do things without her, as still at the age of 14, she would insist on coming into the bathroom while I was in the bath, so she could wash my hair - as I couldn't be trusted to do it myself. She would always take forever too, I would be sat in the bath until it went cold, waiting for her to come and wash my hair. I hated this part of bath time. I was going through puberty and growing into a young woman, the last thing I wanted was my mother in the bathroom with me. As well as washing my hair, she would also pick at my blackheads. She had this metal contraption that was meant to help get the blackheads out easier, but she would dig so deeply into my temples with it, I literally felt like I was going to pass out.

The arrangement I had staying at Katrina's didn't last for as long as I would have liked. I think there was some disagreement between my mother and Katrina, so I had to go back home. Back to the chores of dishes and having to iron Kiara and Kevin's school uniforms. I hated that I had to do so much, my mother didn't work and there was always a whole day's worth of dishes to do in the evenings.

Some days, I would have so much homework to do, I would rush through the dishes, so they wouldn't be cleaned properly. I learnt my lesson of cutting corners when I came home to the dirty dishes in my bed. My mother unmade my bed, put the dirty dishes under the covers and then made the bed back over them, if I hadn't done them properly. Despite having to do so much as a teenager, I was never given pocket money. I only got it for two weeks, then Mike and I got into an argument one day and my mother said that was the end of pocket money. I didn't care though; I was on free school meals and would get £1 a day for anything extra, so I would save my £1 and at the end of the month I would have £20 of my own.

My time staying at Katrina's had made my mother loosen the reins on me slightly, she also let my friend Mel stay round as well. I think she liked her because she called her "Aunty D" and because she used to do the washing up; as long as my mother didn't have to do the dishes, she was happy. I can count on one hand the amount of times I saw my mother doing housework. Mel was always at my house, so she was aware of my mother's unusual personality. It was nice to have someone I didn't have to pretend around. I was even allowed to stay at Mel's house occasionally, which was usually such an effort to get my mother to agree to with anyone else.

Leading up to my 13th birthday, my Grandmother came to stay with us for a while. It was easier for her to stay with us as my mother was the only one out of herself and my aunts that didn't have a job. Things were particularly bad with me and Kiara at this point; she was a real mouthy kid. The two of us never stopped arguing and of course, with me being the older one I would get in trouble. My Grandmother tried to stick up for me, but it just resulted in her and my mother arguing.

The night before my birthday, my Grandmother saw how upset I was and tried to cheer me up. My mother overheard her saying stuff about her and she kicked off. I lay there that night thinking about how much my birthday would be ruined by this. My mother was giving me the silent treatment, after she had told me I could leave with my Grandmother - who was also getting the silent treatment. In the morning the tension in the house was noticeable by everyone. The arguments started again and my mother gave my Grandmother her marching orders. I sat there and watched as she packed her things. She hesitated, and you could hear the pain in her voice when she said to my mother "well, I'm leaving now." It was like she was waiting for my mother to say she had changed her mind; she didn't. My Grandmother left, I looked out of the window, it was pouring with rain and my heart felt heavy as I watched her walk into the distance, with her head down dragging her suitcase behind her.

My mother was still a ticking bomb; if not more than ever. The arguments between her and Mike were unbearable; I often found myself comforting Kiara and Kevin during a heated argument. My mother would kick Mike out, and we would have to listen to hours of him begging for her to open the door. He would make excuse after excuse to come in, he needed the toilet or he needed a drink. My mother would eventually let him in on the condition that he left again after, but we all knew this wouldn't happen and the arguments would just continue.

Our house was becoming extremely overcrowded. My mother had accumulated a number of possessions over the years, and we now lived in a hoarder's house. From the moment you stepped through the door, there was clutter everywhere. You would have to side walk down the narrow hallway, so you would not trip on anything. The kitchen table was always piled high, full of ironing and other rubbish that had been collected there over time. My mother's room was the worst of the lot, I don't remember the last time you could actually see her bedroom floor. It was jam-packed full of clothes, paperwork and other random items. She never put her clothes away in a wardrobe; there was a mountain of clothes on the floor.

Kiara and Kevin were also still sharing a bed in my mother's room. Kiara must have been about 5 or 6 before she actually got her own bed. My mother finally decided she needed more space and Kiara came in to share with me. I was 14 years old at this time; the last thing I wanted to do was share a room with my little sister, but of course, I knew due to our situation, I had no choice. My room started to become cluttered with toys and I hated bringing anyone around.

Despite the state of the house, my room had still been guest friendly. I would take my friends straight to my room and wouldn't let them go anywhere else other than the bathroom. Now that I had to share, my mother started to add her clutter to my room, claiming it was my sister's stuff. I never let her take up more than a small space, where I allowed her to put a pile of her stuff in my room. Every so often, she would add something to her pile and I would throw something away from the bottom, so that she wouldn't notice. She had that much clutter, she really didn't notice. Ever.

There was one time I was allowed to have a sleepover; I invited three friends over, and made sure the living room was tidy enough for us all to take over for the night. My mother left us to it and was actually quite well behaved. She usually started shouting at someone when we had guests. We did the typical teenage things most girls our age were doing at sleepovers - spoke about boys, played truth or dare and 'He said, she said,' which is where you would write part of a story, fold it over and pass it on to the next person. This would keep going until everyone had written a name for a boy and a girl, where they met and what they did. It was always a funny game to play, as you could never predict the outcome. The next morning, the girls left to go home and I tidied up all the sleepover mess. I scrunched up all the bits of paper we had used for our game, and threw them in the bin in my bedroom.

The next day at school, the girls and I talked about the sleepover, how much fun it was, and arranged when to do it again. At lunch time, I received a call from my mother. As soon as I answered the phone she started shouting at me. I had no idea what she was saying, until I realised she had read our 'He said, she said' stories. What we had written wasn't even that bad. It was about kissing boys and having babies. It was totally innocent. She wasn't happy, even after I explained it was just a game. She was adamant that it was the last sleepover I'd ever have and that I was grounded for a week. She hung up and I took in what had just happened. I had just been grounded for a silly teenage game and then I realised. *Why was she going through my bin anyway?*

Seeing how much she overreacted, I decided to never indulge in conversations about boys and relationships with my mother. Or anything personal really; I couldn't even speak to my mother about normal things like periods. I had so many questions. She only ever bought us pads to use. One time I asked her about tampons and she shut the conversation down, saying that they are dangerous, they would give me a toxic shock and I'd die, so I never asked about them again. It wasn't until I was in my twenties that I actually found out how to use them properly from a friend of mine, but even then, I was sceptical of them, as I had the "you will die" conversation in the back of my head.

As I got to the age of getting ready for my GCSEs, it was very hard for me to study in the house. There was endless arguing, kids running around and being kids, and me being moaned at to do the dishes and iron the kids uniforms. I tried so hard to concentrate, but it was impossible. I used to sit at my computer just wishing I could get away from it all. I sat there for hours on MSN and MySpace; it was a getaway from my reality.

Thank god for technology like this to keep me sane! I could finally block my mother out whilst she stood at my bedroom door shouting at me, typing away on MSN "I hate this woman" allowed me to release the anger that was building up. I had started to become more and more isolated from my family, and kept myself very much to myself. My mother had no boundaries and I wasn't allowed any privacy, I had a curtain as a door, at the age of 16. If I was on the phone with someone my mother would come and sit in the room with me and listen to my conversation, like it was her right. She was still invading my bath times too, I had no privacy, except for MSN. I tried really hard to get on with revision, but I just couldn't concentrate in that house. One day, I lit my candles and put my music on to try and focus. It didn't work. I was still yelled at to do the dishes and moaned at to turn my music off, because Kiara needed to go to bed.

When I wasn't online distracting myself from the reality of my life, I liked to bake cakes. I found something very therapeutic about cooking. My mother never let me cook meals though, she would always tell me I didn't know how to do things, and that she would do it herself. One time, I was preparing a salad when my mother came in and told me I was doing it wrong. She told me to get out of the way and let her do it. I snapped back and told her to just leave me to get on with it.

As she continued to argue with me, she went to grab the knife from me, I pulled it away and told her again to let me get on with it. Before I knew it there was blood all over the salad, as I had pulled away, she grabbed the blade and I had sliced straight through her palm, running between her forefinger and thumb. I panicked, as she told me not to say a word to anyone about what had happened. She called Mike to take her to the hospital and I sat at home waiting to find out what was going on. Was I going to get arrested for stabbing my mother, was that why she told me not to tell anyone. She messaged me from the hospital, letting me know she may have to have surgery as I cut through her nerve. She told me that if I told anyone what had happened I would be in serious trouble. She told everyone that the knife slipped as she was preparing the salad and she cut herself trying to grab it. She had made me believe that I would be in serious trouble for this obvious accident, and she used that incident to blackmail me for months.

Despite my lack of preparation for my exams, I managed to get through them with some pretty decent grades and I made it into sixth form so was delighted that I was able to do my A levels.

CHAPTER 10
ENTANGLED IN A MOTHER'S WEB OF CHAOS

The summer holiday after my exams was one of the first summers where I actually had a lot to do. Everyone was on a high from finishing their exams, and we were all ready to celebrate. I had to plan things right if I wanted to go out, I had to choose a moment where my mother was in a good mood. Even though, most of the time when I asked if I could go out, she wasn't happy about it. She would say things like "do what you want." It was her way of saying "I don't want you to go and if you know what's good for you, then you won't go." I was no longer scared of her craziness. I wanted to go or I wouldn't have asked; this was my logic, so I would do exactly as she said, and do what I wanted.

There was one time I asked to stay at a friend's house. My mother was fine with me going, but the next morning she texted me at 7.30am to tell me that I had forty five minutes to get home. Considering that most of my friends lived near my school, which was 7 miles away from my house, this wasn't realistic. Being a normal 16 year old, I wasn't up at 7:30am to see these messages from her. I was woken up by my phone vibrating as she kept ringing, I jumped up and saw ten missed calls.

I knew I was going to get it for this. I went to the bathroom, so I could call her back without waking up my friend. My mother screamed that I now had fifteen minutes to get home, otherwise that sleepover would be the last thing I ever did. When my friend's parents realised I was leaving so early they were really confused. They tried to convince me to stay a bit longer, so they could make breakfast for me. I had to make the decision to stay and deal with my mother's wrath or to leave and come across as rude to my friend's parents. Just then my phone rang again and I knew what I had to do. As soon as I got home, I got the silent treatment. It would be a while before I could ask about doing anything else.

When I started sixth form, I pretty much kept myself to myself when it came to interacting with my mother. I only told her the bare minimum.

I was quite open about my relationship with my mother with my closest friends however, they all knew how crazy she was. They offered great comfort when she was having one of her episodes, and whenever they saw me randomly burst into tears in the library, after receiving a ton of abusive messages from her. Not long into my first year of A Levels, my mother suspected that Mike was having an affair. She asked me to log into his online mobile phone records and print off every single one of his phone bills. She then got me to go through and highlight this one number that came up a lot. She discovered that some of these calls were made late at night.

She started going mental, I knew that as soon as he got home that would be it, I was right! It all kicked off, she threw the phone bills at him and started shouting all kinds of abuse at him. Kiara and Kevin were crying, they were scared. I went into their room and hugged them until it stopped. The trouble with my mother, was that she always aired her dramas to us. We shouldn't have even been involved. She came into the room and told Kiara and Kevin that their father would be leaving because he's a cheater. They argued for hours and hours. It ended with the usual locking out of the house and him begging to come back in.

The arguments went on for weeks. It was like living in a nightmare. My mother decided that she wanted us to move out of London. We got into an argument about it, because I didn't want to go. I was in the middle of my A Levels. The last thing I wanted to do was move away with her to somewhere I knew nobody. She told me that I was selfish and that it always had to be about me, yet her making us move was all about her. She didn't understand that you cannot just uproot during such important exams. She said she was going to go without me and I could sort something out for myself. Trying to study for your A Levels with all of this stress on your shoulders is not an ideal situation, to say the least.

A few weeks later, things went back to normal. I noticed that my mother never spoke about things. She liked to brush everything under the carpet and act like nothing happened. During this time, I'd started dog sitting for a woman named June. Her daughter went to the same school as Kiara and Kevin and that's how we met. I loved spending time with June and her family; they were so normal compared to ours.

June was the kind of mother I had always dreamed of. I used to talk to June a lot about my mother, she gave me such sensible advice. She never made me feel bad like other people did. I was so used to being told "But, she's your mother, she loves you really, you only get one mother in life." It was something new for me to have an adult that actually listened and gave real guidance. I learnt a lot about myself from June.

When it was time to start applying for Universities, I had my heart set on Roehampton University. It wasn't too far from home and it had a really good reputation for teaching courses. I had wanted to go there since I'd started looking at Universities. My mother thought that we should look at other places as well. I didn't want to. Truth was, if I didn't go to Roehampton, I didn't want to go anywhere else. She forced me to go and look at Winchester University; we argued and argued at how much I hated the look of this University, yet my mother went ahead and booked the train tickets for us to go to the open day.

After she booked the tickets, I expressed again how unhappy I was about going, we got into another argument; this time, because she said that I should have told her I didn't want to go. She couldn't be serious? Had she not been listening to the numerous times I had told her that I didn't want to go? The argument ended with her telling me I was ungrateful, then I got the silent treatment for the rest of the day. I decided to save myself from all these arguments. She clearly liked to make things more difficult, so I vowed to just keep my mouth shut on this topic.

I couldn't wrap my head around my mother wanting me to move away to Winchester, when the latest fight with her was about her not wanting me to live out if I went to Roehampton. I agreed that if I got accepted to Roehampton, then I would stay at home in order to save money. She seemed happy with this and there was no more said about it. I was soon to turn 18 years old and was so excited at what this freedom would bring me. My A Level exams were over and I focused on getting myself a job, so that I had some money to spend over the summer, celebrating all my other friends turning 18 and of course celebrating our exam results.

CHAPTER 11
THE JOURNEY TO INDEPENDENCE

The day I turned 18, my mother eased off a bit. When I asked to go out, she was happy and didn't even question the time I was coming home. This was too good to be true!

When the day came to collect my A Level results, I was so nervous! I suddenly realised just how much I wanted to get into University, I started to worry that I wouldn't get the results I needed. My mother was still asleep when I left that morning to collect my results. I was hoping she would be up to wish me luck or offer some words of support. Who was I kidding? That was too much to ask for. So, off I went to find out what my next step in life would be. It is such a crazy feeling to not know for months if you will be going to University or not! Your life is in limbo until you open that envelope.

I held the envelope in my hand and looked around. So many people had their parents with them, some were crying; some with happiness, some with disappointment. This made me even more nervous, as some of my smartest friends were crying, and were frantically trying to go through clearing to get accepted into alternative universities. I opened my results. I had no idea what they meant or if I had been offered a place, so I logged onto the website and that's when I saw it "Congratulations! You have been accepted!" I started screaming. I did it! I got into University. It was two hours after I had left home before my mother contacted me. She sent a text message simply saying "Well.." I messaged back telling her I got in and she replied "That's good." I don't know what more I expected from her really! She had never shown any emotion, so why would she start now?

On my way home from getting my results, I bumped into June. She was so excited when she saw me and could not wait to find out about my results. This was the kind of reaction I had hoped for from my mother. June said she would throw a BBQ to celebrate my results and that she would ring my mother and tell her to come over. June went all out; she made jugs of Pimms and really tried to enthuse my mother to have the same excitement as she did. If I am honest, I would have preferred if my mother was not there. Her miserable sour face was putting a downer on my happiness, and made me feel uncomfortable. When June's husband came home, he expressed the same excitement as she had. June came over with a candle lit cake singing "Congratulations to you." I was so overwhelmed that I started to cry. These people, who had been in my life for just under a year, were more excited about me getting into University than my own mother.

Over time, my mother began to grow extremely jealous of how close June and I had become. We were always getting into arguments that ended in my mother saying "sorry I'm not June." Truth is I would have loved it if she was; or even just more like any normal mother, one who actually loved her children.

During the summer leading up to me starting at University, I worked most of the time as a waitress in a pub, which meant I didn't need to ask my mother for anything. I had my own money. I really wanted to live out when I went to University, but my mother was still against the idea. I decided I would claim the full student loan just in case, despite my mother having a problem with this too.

The day finally came for me to start University. It didn't quite feel how I had imagined. I had watched so many movies where people had gone off to University, but without the whole living in dorms part, it just didn't feel right. It was a lot harder to make friends when you commuted every day, so I only knew a small handful of people from my course. There was one plus side to living at home - all the money I saved. This meant that for a student, I did have a lot of money left over.

I had become obsessed with shopping. I would buy the same pair of shoes in three different colours. It was like a release for me, something my mother couldn't control, although she still had a lot to say about this and it resulted in regular arguments. To save myself the headache, I left items at June's house, only taking home what I could hide in my bag. June was becoming more and more of a saviour. If I ever wanted some peace and quiet to get on with my coursework, I would tell my mother I was babysitting for June and would stay at her house for the night. I cannot tell you how heavenly it was to be able to do my work without someone constantly moaning and shouting at you.

I would be sat in an armchair in the corner of June's living room, with my headphones on working away on my laptop. Although I couldn't hear what was being said, I would look up and see June, her husband and their daughter all snuggled on the sofa, laughing together and it made me smile. I had never had that. It made me feel all fuzzy inside, just seeing a loving family. I don't think they will ever realise how grateful I am for moments like these.

They gave me hope and made me realise that there is real love out there. To feel so loved and cared for myself in that environment, I knew it wasn't my fault the way my mother was with me. Other people were able to love me, so it couldn't be me.

Another get away for me was to visit my friend in Guildford. Despite me being an adult, it didn't make my mother ease off. During a stay in Guildford, there was a train strike and I could not get home the next morning. My friend's sister was visiting too, so she said she would give me a lift back to London in the evening. I rang my mother to let her know and she went mad. She started shouting at me, saying I should have checked the trains before to make sure they were running.

I did not understand what her problem was; I would still be home by 7pm that evening. I received messages with abuse from my mother all day, telling me that if I wasn't back on time she'd lock the doors. At 7pm, like she had an alarm set, she rang to see where I was. We had left Guildford later than planned, so I didn't get home until around 9pm. As soon as I walked in through the door, I got the usual "you aren't going anywhere else again." I had learnt to not argue with my mother anymore. I just called her all the names under the sun in my head.

CHAPTER 12
SACRIFICED BONDS

My first year of University drew to an end and things at home weren't any better. The arguments between my mother and Mike continued and she told my siblings and me on a regular basis how much she hated him. One thing I was looking forward to about the summer holidays was that I was going to be house-sitting for 3 weeks. Fantastic! A 3-week break from the hell hole I called home.

A few days before I was due to leave for my housesit I decided to pack a suitcase. I had never been so excited to get away. We never went on holidays, except for when we went to Portugal when I was 12 years old, so this break was more exciting than most would have found it. The thought of being able to sleep in without the fear of being woken up to Britney Spears' *Toxic* playing really loud, or being pushed out of the kitchen because I woke up late and wasn't allowed to make breakfast after 12pm; these were the things I was most excited about.

My mother was acting strange over the last few days before my housesit; she had become very secretive and shifty. One morning, around 7am, she told me she was helping my Aunt move house, but she was back within an hour. I questioned her about where she had been, she was just laughing and mumbled how she couldn't tell me. I joked and said "What? Are you pregnant or something?" She didn't say anything, so I carried on the joke and shouted to Kiara and Kevin "Mum is having a baby". My mother turned to me and said "I didn't want to tell them yet!"

Wait? Was she serious? She was pregnant? I was so confused. She was always going on about how much she hated Mike, and now she was pregnant. I didn't know how to take this in. I started lecturing her about contraception. Why did I suddenly feel like I was the adult in this conversation? My mother was 6 weeks pregnant the day we found out, and she used it as an excuse for not doing things around the house.

The night before leaving for my housesit my mother and Mike had been shopping. When they got home Mike started shouting at me because I hadn't done the dishes yet. I was working on an essay I had to complete over the summer. I was over all of his moaning about washing up, he always expected it to be done as soon as we had finished eating. I didn't see the problem in it being left for a while after, it was still going to get done and it's not like we had an immaculate house.

He went on and on; something had clearly annoyed him that evening. I ignored him until he threw in the "you need to help out more now that your mother is pregnant."

I saw red and lashed out, "I'm not the one that got her pregnant!" This hit a nerve. He came at me like he was going to hit me, he was screaming in my face, saying he was going to knock my teeth out. He had his fist clenched, and his nostrils were flared. I saw the anger in his eyes, and as much as it scared me, I dared him to do it. I pointed at my mouth while I held the phone in my other hand, to call the police if he did.

He backed down and said "Why don't you go and find your real father?" He knew this would get to me. I pushed him out of the way, called him a few names and ran out of the house.

I was so upset, I didn't stop to think before I left, so I had no shoes or jacket on and it was midnight. I had no idea what I was going to do. I hated both of them. How could my mother stand by and let him behave that way towards me? If anyone ever raised their hand to my child, I would kill them. Why was I surprised? It's not like she had ever shown her caring side in the past. It took my mother almost two hours to text me.

"Are you coming back or what? I want to lock the door."

I stared at the phone in disbelief, she had no idea where I was or if I was okay. It cut me deep that evening how little she cared for me. My heart had never been this heavy before. I replied back saying that I would not be coming home if Mike was there, she told me he was going to bed and that she would talk to him in the morning. Considering I had no other options, I went back. I was in a state and my mother didn't say anything to me, she went straight to bed and shouted for me to lock the door. That night as I lay there crying, contemplating if I wanted to live this life anymore, I decided to write a letter to my mother.

"Mum, I know I haven't been the perfect daughter recently and I am sorry. But I have to let all these things out, because I will just make myself ill. When I ran out of the house last night, I did a lot of thinking and I'm fed up with the way Mike treats me. He has threatened me too many times over the years, and up until now it has never bothered me, but if you had seen the anger in his eyes, he actually meant it this time. If I didn't walk out I would have hit him. It's not good for someone to make me feel so much hate! He's messing up my head!

If I hadn't have walked out without any shoes on, I would have carried on walking and God knows where I would have ended up or what would have happened to me. I meant it when I said I will help you look after this baby, but as long as Mike is living under this roof, I can't. I can't live somewhere that makes me think if I just slit my throat it will all be over and you can all carry on playing happy families.

So, while I'm away for these next three weeks you can think about this and if you decide to ignore all I'm saying, I will walk away forever and you will never see me again. I don't want to, but if that's what it takes, I will. I can't live like this anymore! As your daughter, I am asking you to make the right choice.

We both know I can't afford to move out, but if it means living on the streets, then so be it. Take these three weeks to think, I won't be coming home during this time, but if you want to see me you know where I am.

Lots of love, Kylie."

My head was all over the place. Looking back, maybe I did go a bit over the top. I was blinded by my mother's behaviour and blamed Mike for everything, or maybe I just wanted to feel loved by my mother and this was a cry for help? I knew that the pain I was feeling was valid. Surely my mother, the woman who had expressed her hatred for Mike for so many years would choose me, her daughter. Right?

I felt better for getting everything off my chest and was able to get some sleep. The next morning, I was still really upset by the previous night's antics, so I decided the letter was still a good idea. I gave it to my mother and waited for a response. I could hear my mother whispering to Mike; I am not sure what she said but I guessed it wasn't nice considering he replied "What, you would actually do that?" My mother responded saying "I really don't care anymore." It felt like someone had ripped my heart out and thrown it into a blender. I got my suitcase and I left. Before I left, I went into my mother and said "I guess this is goodbye then." She said nothing, so I left. I cried the whole way there. I felt like my life was over. My whole world was crumbling around me and I had no idea what I was going to do.

When I arrived at the empty house I would be staying in for the next 3 weeks, I felt so lonely. I sat in the middle of the floor crying so much it hurt. I cried so much that I made myself sick. I was drained. I contemplated ending it then and there. My phone rang. It was my cousin Lola. She had rung to see how I was settling into my freedom. She realised that something was wrong and spoke to me for hours until she was sure I was okay. She always knew how to lift my spirits and she gave great advice.

The next day I felt a bit better. I hadn't heard from my mother, but I decided to make the most of my time away and this new-found freedom. I arranged to meet a few friends and went out and forgot about everything for a while. A few days had gone by and I still had not heard from my mother. This upset me. I missed my brother and sister and I thought I would never see them again.

I started applying for loads of jobs, preparing for having to survive on my own. This had always scared me in the past as my mother constantly told me I did not have the life skills to manage in the real world. Since I had been housesitting I was starting to realise this wasn't entirely true. I had not burnt the house down, I had not given myself food poisoning and I was managing my budget quite well. A week had passed before I heard from my mother, shocking considering the last time I saw her, I had given her a letter telling her I wanted to kill myself.

My mother rang me to tell me I had post and she started going on about me being really selfish. I had only just managed to get back into a happy place so I told her I needed to go and I hung up. A few more days went by when my mother said we should meet up in the park, so we could have a chat. I agreed. Kiara and Kevin would be there too and I really missed them. When I met them, it was very awkward. Kiara and Kevin went to play in the playground while my mother and I sat on the grass outside with the dog. I didn't say anything for a bit. My mother sat there picking daisies saying nothing. I didn't know what to say. We needed to talk about what happened, rather than brush it under the carpet like we usually do. I was scared to mention it in case it sent my mother into the ticking time bomb again. She broke the silence, talking about the baby and how tired it was making her. We didn't speak about much else and before I knew it my mother was ready to leave. She had to get the kids home for their dinner. So we said goodbye.

I walked away still very confused about the outcome of the meet up. Had it helped? Had we discussed the issue? Would I be going home? I had so many unanswered questions. My mother was never one to say sorry, or speak about her emotions. Maybe this was her way of saying everything was okay for me to come home now? I went to sleep with such a headache that evening, tossing and turning through most of the night, going over and over these questions in my head.

The next day, I was feeling a bit better. Then my cousin Lola rang me. She said she was only ringing because she thought I had the right to know, in order for me to prepare for what was about to happen. I became worried, wondering what she could possibly tell me that could be worse than anything I had experienced in the last week. She informed me that she had been to visit my mother and she had packed up all my stuff and was planning the colour scheme for what was my bedroom - she was going to kick me out.

My heart sank. It was suddenly all real. What was I going to do? I started to regret writing the letter; should I have just continued to live in hell and carried on as if nothing had happened? This wasn't all though, Lola also told me that my mother had hacked into my Facebook account and had read all my private messages. I was absolutely livid. I had spent this last week discussing the issue with my friends via Facebook. This was a time before WhatsApp, when everyone's main form of communication was Facebook Messenger and I had private conversations on there of things my mother didn't know about. There was no way I could live in the same house as this woman now. This was the biggest betrayal to date. I could not believe that she could stoop so low. It was yet another invasion of my privacy.

I decided not to let on to my mother about what Lola had told me. I instantly changed all my passwords on all social media accounts and I put my name down on the list for student accommodation at my University. I was distraught and being the lost, confused teenager I was, I decided to drink until I passed out to help numb what I was feeling.

I had a week and a half left to figure out what I was going to do. I decided not to panic and told myself that something would work out. I always tried to use this way of thinking, after I had got over the initial worrying stage. Just like that the calls started to come through from the accommodation list. I received a call from a girl called Danni about viewing a house share. It was a 5 minute walk from my University and it sounded perfect. I agreed to go the next day.

CHAPTER 13
IS THIS WHAT FREEDOM FEELS LIKE?

I was excited about moving out, I had accepted that this was the next step for me. And it was going to be the best thing moving forward. As I followed the directions to the flat I was going to view, I started to discover a part of my University I had never seen before. It was dark and dreary and had a cold feel to it. As I walked deeper into an estate, I started to wonder what this walk would be like in the heart of winter or coming home after a night out. I did not feel safe at all.

When I arrived at the flat, I walked into the building and up the stairs. The block was even worse than the street. The stairs smelled of urine and there were beer cans and cigarette butts everywhere. The walls were covered in graffiti. I passed a group of boys hanging around on the stairs whistling at me. I instantly made my mind up about this flat. Inside, the flat was lovely, but I couldn't live somewhere I felt so unsafe. I headed back after the viewing feeling deflated. I only had three days left of my housesit and still did not know what I was going to do.

I was in panic mode again. Just when I was going to give up hope, I received a call about a viewing the day before my housesit was due to come to an end. The girl on the phone said "I know it's really short notice but we need someone to come and meet us tomorrow with the view of moving in next week". My prayers had been answered, I arranged to meet the girls the next day and I prayed this viewing would be better than my last.

The next morning, I arrived at the flat. It was on a ground floor, very well-lit and closer to the University than the other property. It had the exact layout as the other flat, however I had the option of an upstairs bedroom. I met two of the girls: Saskia and Christen. They were lovely and I accepted the room. We arranged to meet the landlord in two days to sign the contracts. I could not believe how this had all worked out! Just 3 weeks previously, I was at home, with my mother, not knowing what I was going to do and now I was about to sign a contract to move out.

The next morning, the owners of the house I was watching returned. They were already aware of some of the issues I had with my mother, so I filled them in on what had happened over the past 3 weeks. They were extremely supportive and said that I could stay in the spare room until I moved. This was a great help for me. I was going for a long weekend to Dublin, so I would only really need to stay there for three nights. It was so overwhelming for me that complete strangers could show more love towards me than my own mother.

I needed to go home to get some stuff for Dublin. I made my cousin Lucy come with me, so I wouldn't have to face my mother alone. You could cut the tension with a knife when I walked in. I went into my bedroom and saw all my stuff was indeed packed up and the walls had paint samples on. I took a deep breath and started sorting out stuff that I needed for Dublin.

I think my mother was expecting me to beg her not to kick me out or to be upset about my room being packed up. But I had been prepared for this, so I kept it together. She came in and saw me sorting things out. She quickly got angry.

"Don't think you can just come here and start making a mess after I tidied up!"

When had my mother ever tidied up and when did packing all my belongings into boxes count as tidying up? I stayed calm and turned to her.

"I am not making a mess. I am packing what I need."

Her face dropped. Her plan backfired. She wanted to break me, but instead I was stronger than ever when I hit her with my comeback.

"Oh, did I forget to tell you? I'm moving out."

She paused for a second. I had never known my mother to be lost for words. She finally caught her words and said, "Whatever, you need to be careful what you tell people, because I know stuff about you!"

Again I kept my cool. "You only know stuff because you hacked my Facebook. *You* need to be careful who you talk to because I know things too."

With that said, I had set off a ticking time bomb. She started screaming at me saying that if I left I would never be allowed to come back. I don't think she realised I had already left. She was still hurling abuse at me as I was walking out of the door. I needed to get out of there quick! I was scared, but I was also on adrenaline high.

"Fuck you!" I shouted as I slammed the door as hard as I could. I was shaking when I left, my heart was racing, I couldn't believe that I had just sworn at my mother and got out alive. I had done it. I had survived the wrath of my mother. For the first time in my life I was the one in control. I had stood up to her and I felt free!

Everything was working out great, I met with the girls to sign the contracts and pay the deposits for the house. I was so lucky to have somewhere to stay until then, and I could not wait for my break away to Dublin. I was finally going to be given the independence to find myself.

The night before I was due to go to Dublin, I messaged my mother to let her know that she would soon get what she wanted and that I would be gone and all I needed from her was for her to sign my guarantor.

She rang me that evening and was quite upset. I have never known her to show emotion like this. She asked me to come back home and said we could work through this. I explained how after everything that had happened, I felt like it was too late to go back. It had been almost a month since the fight with Mike and when I handed her the letter. Yet, she wanted to try and work things out now? I had cried out for her weeks ago and she was the one that packed up my things. She told me that she was going to get rid of the baby as she knew this was the reason I was "acting out."

This set me off. I had been calm the whole conversation, until that moment. *How dare she try and put that on me?* Such thoughts had never crossed my mind. I told her I would never forgive her if she got rid of the baby and used me as a reason. This was the most messed up thing my mother had ever suggested. I hung up on her and cried myself to sleep that night. I could not believe that my mother would try and pin an abortion on me.

I was so glad to be going to Dublin. I needed a few days to get my head around everything, sure I was excited about moving, but I was feeling very anxious. My whole life was about to change. I was still really distraught about the last conversation I had with my mother as well.

While I was in Dublin my mother rang me. She said she was struggling to sign the guarantor and felt as if she was signing her life away. I needed her to sign that form. The other girls were supposed to be moving in just a few days and if my mother had not signed that form they wouldn't be able to. She was not just ruining things for me, but also for them. I was stood outside the bar I was at, going back and forth with her for hours about this. We got into another fight and she said I was no longer her daughter, and that she never wanted to see me again. I told her if that was true, then she would not find a problem in signing the form. I thought Dublin would be a break for me, but there I was crying my heart out again because of my mother.

The next day my mother rang back. She had calmed down. She said she had signed the form and that she wanted me to come home when I got back from Dublin. She promised she would not argue with me, and that she would help me pack my stuff properly. I agreed to go back. I was confused, all these weeks, she had made things so difficult for me, then all of a sudden she was being nice again. I tried to enjoy the rest of my break in Dublin, but I was still sceptical whether my mother would actually stick to her promise. At least I knew the guarantor had been signed.

When I got back from Dublin, my mother did actually stick to her word, and helped me pack without any stress. It was nice to actually have the help of a mother for the first time in my life. I could tell she was upset that I was moving out, but there was nothing she could do to stop it now and it was definitely for the best.

The day finally came! Everything happened so suddenly, I was extremely nervous. My lifetime possessions had been packed into one small van and I was off. And within a few hours, I was standing alone in my new bedroom surrounded by cases and boxes of unpacking. A sense of joy filled up inside me. This was my new start, it could only get better from here.

It did not take me long to settle into my new home. I was loving everything about it. I started to find that my relationship with my mother was actually improving since I moved out. She did not argue with me anymore. However, three weeks into my new found freedom, it all took a turn for the worse. One night, after returning from a party with my housemates, we came home to find the house had been broken into. I remember it like it was yesterday. As I walked up the stairs and saw my room ransacked, my legs gave in, and I fell to the floor screaming "We've been burgled."

It was 5am and I rang my mother in a state. She answered instantly, suspecting something was wrong. It didn't take long for Mike and her to turn up to the house. My mother was ranting on and on, saying she knew something like this was going to happen and that she should have never let me leave. Everything she said after that was a blur to me. I had been awake for almost 24 hours. All I wanted was to wake up and realise that this was all a horrible dream. My mother took me back to her house and I was still in shock. Everything had been going so well up until then; this was not how it was supposed to end. I had nightmares for nights after that, and my mother was insisting that I move back with her. I was not going to let this incident affect how far I had come. There was no way I could move back. I picked myself up and I was determined to make it work.

When I returned to the house, I freaked out a little. I was the only one home so I arranged to meet one of my housemates in the library. It took me a while before I could be there alone; I never slept in the house alone though. I would always go to my mother's on the weekend if no one else was home, and I insisted the hallway light was left on every night.

Six months after I moved, my mother gave birth to my brother, Kane. He was perfect and from that moment on, I promised to be the best big sister I could. After he was born, I spent most of my time going back and forth to my mother's house. I wanted to spend as much time with Kane as I could. Shortly after he was born, I started to struggle at University. I would spend endless nights in the library, trying to get work done.

After a week of 5am library stretches, I broke down. I could not find it in myself to make it through my course. All of my friends tried to convince me to see it through to the end of 2nd year. I couldn't force myself to continue with something I really wasn't enjoying and was making me so unhappy. I rang my mother to tell her how I was feeling, and I was shocked to find that she agreed with me. She said that I had been miserable over the last few months and that I should do what made me happy.

I had never really been an academic person. I learnt through doing, so with that said, it was final and I dropped out. I still had four months left on my tenancy agreement, so I carried on living the life of a student for those final months and I decided to get a job and try to find somewhere else to live when it ended. It proved a lot harder to find somewhere to live this time around. So the only option I had left was to move back to my mother's until I could find somewhere else. I didn't think things would be that bad seeing as our relationship had improved a lot since I moved out and Kane was born.

CHAPTER 14
BACK HERE AGAIN?

When I moved back to my mother's, most of my stuff was still packed up and had to stay in the hall as I was sharing a room with Kiara and Kevin. I had a corner in their room to place some of my things, but it was terribly overcrowded. I had just spent the last year living in complete freedom, and now at the age of 20, I was sharing with my 11 and 12 year old siblings. When I wasn't at work, I tried to spend as much time as possible out of the house. It was difficult sharing with my younger siblings. I had to be quiet when they went to bed, and they would moan if I had the lamp on while they were trying to sleep.

After almost a year of living back at my mother's, I was starting to get fed up. My job wasn't paying half as much as I needed to be able to move out, and I wasn't saving much as I had to give my mother £300 a month for rent and spent the rest trying to be out of the house as much as possible. Looking back, I'm not sure why she was charging me so much to have a bed in the corner of my sibling's room. It's almost like this was her way of keeping me at home.

There was one night, I decided to go to my old manager, Natalie's birthday meal. The weather was horrendous. The scene outside was almost comparable to the storm from 'The Wizard of Oz.' I was determined to get out of that house though. My mother could not understand why I was going to go out in that weather for someone that I hardly knew. I just needed to do it though, I wasn't sure why at the time, but I knew I needed to.

After Natalie's birthday I discovered that John, my Aunty Angela's boyfriend, was her Uncle. From that moment on we were inseparable. Natalie became my best friend, a best friend like no other, it had taken me 21 years but I had finally found a friend that I could rely on no matter what. Natalie became my rock. She was the one I confided in about my mother. For years, no one really understood and whenever I even tried to talk to them about my relationship with my mother they would interrupt with the famous words "but she's your mum." Natalie allowed me to pour my heart out, and she never judged.

My mother hated that I had someone to turn to. I would be at Natalie's house and get calls from my mother to come home. I was 21 years old and I was being treated like a child. One night, she rang and said that if I didn't come home, then to not bother coming back the next day. I was so fed up with all her controlling. I broke down to Natalie so badly, that she cried from just seeing the heartache my mother was causing me. I knew at that point that as long as I had her by my side, I would be able to face anything when it came to my mother.

My mother then started to get annoyed with the time I would get home after work, she would ring me and say if I wasn't home by 7pm she would lock the door and throw away my dinner. I felt like a prisoner. 21 years old, and I was on a curfew. I started to lie to my mother and tell her that I was doing overtime, so that I could meet Natalie after work. We would laugh and joke about me being 'grounded.'

Things at home were becoming harder and harder. My mother and I were constantly arguing about how I treated the place like a hotel. She could not understand how difficult it was to be put under such ridiculous house rules at my age, especially after having the freedom at University. Even though I was meant to be saving to move out, I needed a break. Natalie and I decided to go on holiday to The Bahamas, as she had family there we could stay with, so we booked a three week holiday and I could not wait to get away from my mother for a while. Of course this caused another argument with her. This time, her problem was with me going away for three weeks with someone I had barely known a month. I told her I was going and there was no more to say about the matter. I was an excellent judge of character, I knew that three weeks away with Natalie would not be a problem.

I had hoped that Natalie and my mother could have formed a relationship, just so that my mother could see how amazing she was, yet I feared introducing someone I cared about so much to my mother when she clearly had a problem with her. My mother did not have good people skills, and I was worried she would make her feelings apparent. Even speaking on the phone to Natalie became a problem. On one occasion, we were getting excited about the holiday, when my mother said "why is she screaming?" I was so embarrassed as Natalie had heard her and I did not want my mother's rude persona to hinder my friendship, but luckily she already knew what my mother was like.

A few months later, the time came to go to The Bahamas. I had the most amazing time ever! Natalie and I did not clash once, just like I knew we wouldn't. The holiday opened my eyes up to what an amazing world was out there, I refused to let my mother hold me back anymore. I vowed to myself to make sure I saw more of this beautiful world.

When I landed back from The Bahamas, I rang my mother to let her know I was back. After three weeks away, the jetlag was kicking in like crazy. I was shattered, I told my mother that I was going to sleep off some of my jetlag at Natalie's house, and would come home the following day. The thought of going back to share a room with Kiara and Kevin with that jetlag was not something I was about to settle for. With Kane being a toddler now as well there was no way I would have gotten any sleep.

My mother screamed at me when I told her this. I had landed less than an hour ago and she was already living up to her usual ways.

"You have been away with this girl for three weeks, don't you think you have spent enough time with her? If you don't come home today, then don't bother coming back."

I told her that I was not having that conversation with her, that I would see her the next day and hung up. I was expecting to receive a whole load of abusive text messages after that, but I didn't. I wasn't going to let her dictate to me anymore. I would go home the next day and deal with whatever she had to throw at me.

Despite me not wanting my mother to get to me, she did. I couldn't sleep as I was worrying about what I was going to go home to, so after having something to eat at Natalie's house, I decided to go home and just soldier through the jet lag. Nothing could have prepared me for what I was about to encounter. I walked into the bedroom to find that my bed had been dismantled. My wall that was once covered in photographs was now bare and some of my stuff had been packed up.

My mother had gone a step too far this time. *When did she even have time to do all of this in just a few hours whilst looking after a toddler?* It was like when I was housesitting all over again. I had too much control and my mother didn't like it. She was trying to take back control and have me beg her. She loved to have me needing her.

I sent a text message to Natalie telling her what had happened, she told me to pack what I needed and to go back to her house. I emptied out the contents of my case and started to fill it with clothes I would need for work. My mother came in and asked me what I was doing. *Was this woman serious?* Was she really asking what I was doing? She had to be sick in the head. "What do you think I'm doing?"

She sat down on my sister's bed and looked me dead in the eyes. "You know, you don't have to leave. We can sort this out."

I looked at her confused and shouted, "You dismantled my bed. How are we supposed to sort this out!?"

She said that if I agreed to not see Natalie anymore, then we could forget all of this. I looked at her stunned. She had to be joking, but the look on her face told me otherwise. She was dead serious and was asking me to choose between her and my best friend. I told her I was not going to make that decision and she shouldn't ask me to. She stuck to her guns.

"It's us or her, and if you choose her you will never see your sister and brothers again."

I zipped up my suitcase and got up. I told her she was crazier than I had ever thought, and that I would never choose her of all people over Natalie. With that said, I left. I couldn't believe what had just happened. My mother couldn't bear to see me happy and wanted to take control of my life again, but now she had Kane to use as a weapon and she knew that would get me where it hurt.

On my way back to Natalie's, I bumped into Kiara and Kevin on their way home from school. They were really happy to see me and I briefly told them what had happened, and that I was going. They looked shocked and upset. It was hard to walk away from them not knowing when I would next see them. It was easier to keep in contact with them as they had phones. Kane, on the other hand, was going to be difficult. However, I couldn't be held to ransom by my mother. I needed to escape, while I had the support network to help me.

When I arrived back at Natalie's house, she was waiting outside for me. As soon as she saw me, she came running down the road. I burst into tears. I didn't know what was going to happen. She helped me inside with my things and I told Natalie and her mother what had happened. They told me not to worry, that I could stay there for as long as I needed, and that they would clear the spare room out for me. I was overwhelmed with gratitude. Natalie and her mother had taken me in without a second thought, whereas my own mother was acting like an ogre. I would never forget this and I would be eternally grateful to them.

CHAPTER 15
IT'S ALL JUST MIND GAMES

I cried myself to sleep every night for weeks after that, not knowing if I would see Kane again was ripping me to shreds. I really don't know what I would have done without Natalie. She helped me more than she will ever know during this time. She was a blessing sent from God. My mother still tried her best to ruin this though, she would send weird messages to Natalie's phone meant for me saying things like, "I never realised what a dirty bitch you are, you are disgusting."

I was so bemused as to why she would send messages like this. Natalie used to laugh them off and say that she knew me better than to let some messages turn her against me. We put the messages down to exactly that, my mother trying to make Natalie think I was a horrible person, almost in hope for her to start wondering what she was getting herself into having me live with her and send me packing. However, like Natalie said, she knew me better than this and my mother's plan failed.

My mother continued to think up ways to cause me stress. She would message me telling me I had until the end of the month to collect my things or she would continue to charge me rent as a storage fee, but whenever I tried to get my things, she made it difficult for me. One day, I went round and got as much as I could. Natalie and her stepfather came to meet me and I put my things in the car. Before I left, my mother gave me one more opportunity to come back but again said I had to cut Natalie out of my life. I just shook my head at her and walked out of the door.

It was almost two months before I saw my siblings again. One of my cousins, Lucy, had gone into hospital and my mother rang to tell me. While at the hospital, my mother started talking to me; she had accepted that I wasn't coming back or choosing her over Natalie, and things just went back to normal. Making up with my mother was always a strange moment for me. We would never discuss the problems we had faced; she would literally just flip a switch and carry on as if nothing had happened. I did not care though, as long as I got to see Kane she could brush a whole world war under the carpet and I wouldn't bat an eyelid.

A couple of months later, I was at my mother's house when she called me into her bedroom. She informed me that she had been claiming government benefits while Mike was living with her. She showed me a letter that said she has to pay back £40,000 and would have to go to court. She started crying, asking me to promise to look after Kane if she went to prison. *My mother was pleading with me to be there if she went into prison.* This woman continued to shock me. Just when I thought she couldn't do anything more than she had already done, she hits me with another bombshell.

Miraculously, my mother managed to get out of paying back the money. I don't know how she managed that, but then again she was a wonderful liar. Shortly after, she announced that Mike and her were getting married. Naturally, when someone tells you they are getting married your first instinct is to feel joy for them, but this was not the case with my mother. I found the whole thing extremely weird. She had been very clear to everyone that knew her, how much she hated Mike. I asked her why she suddenly wanted to get married. I wondered what her reasons were, maybe they had a big heart to heart and have realised that they have huge amounts of love for each other. I never would have predicted her answer would be "for family tax credit, it will be cheaper." Of course, there was always a motive with my mother.

Despite this, the build-up to the wedding was exciting. I had never been to a wedding so I was looking forward to it, and it was the first time all of the family would be together probably since my Granddad died. The actual wedding was a weird one. My mother and Mike got married on a Friday in a registry office and invited most of the family except for my cousin Lola and her mother; who is my mother's sister. This caused an issue, but my mother was always trying to leave someone out. I don't think there has been a time where my mother had been on good terms with every single one of her sisters.

The day itself was very awkward. My mother looked like she had been forced to be there and you won't find one photograph of her smiling or looking happy. Even sitting with all her four children together for a photo was difficult. I was sat next to her but I felt her moving further and further away from me, so those photographs are laughable too. The wedding "reception" wasn't until the Sunday, after Kane's christening, where my mother got back into her wedding dress and walked around making the whole day about her. No one there would have known that day was really about Kane.

My mother had everyone doing everything for the reception, from food to decorations, which was fine, but she didn't make requests in appreciative ways; she was demanding. Natalie's mother made a load of chicken for the reception, even though my mother made no effort with Natalie. I was filled with embarrassment on the day when my mother didn't even say hello to Natalie or her mother, let alone say thank you for the chicken.

There was so much tension at the reception! There was conflict between most family members and it was making me feel really uneasy. I was sitting at the head table, during what felt like the longest speeches ever; every single person from Mike's side of the guests would have to come up and hug both him and my mother, as part of his culture, so this went on forever. I ended up get extremely drunk, so I would not have to deal with all the drama from the family and from the boredom of the hugs. I made a drunken speech saying how happy I was for Mike and my mother and it was the first time I ever saw my mother cry. Her whole wedding she didn't show any emotion, but then again, I had just made a grand gesture, so of course my mother had to match it in front of her audience, which was probably why she shed the tears.

After the wedding, things went back to normal. There was an outbreak of arguments within the family from things that had happened or had been said during the wedding. My mother even had a massive argument with my cousin Lola, she rang me immediately after demanding that I never speak to Lola again.

"If you heard the way she spoke to me you wouldn't want to speak to her again."

I explained to her that whatever was said in the argument was between them and I was not going to disown my cousin for this. Lola was like a big sister to me, one of the people I could rely on in a crisis. There was no way I was going to allow my mother to ruin this.

She was not happy that I was disobeying her. Mike started on me as well, asking me how I could talk to someone who made my mother cry. I sat there wondering if they were both delusional, was he really asking me how I could talk to someone who made my mother cry, when she had been making me cry my whole life? My mother also badmouthed me to Kiara and Kevin. Kiara had always been very opinionated and would start telling me I should be taking our mother's side for the pure fact she was our mother. I didn't hold this against Kiara, because I knew what it was like living in the same household as my mother, being brainwashed to feel hate and anger towards people. I knew that Kiara would eventually grow out of this, just as I had.

My mother started to fall out with everyone after the wedding and she tried to make me follow her grudge. She rang to tell me that my Aunty Sarah had been saying horrible things about me, that Sarah had asked how I was able to work with children, when I had left University with no qualifications to sit on benefits. That was far from the truth. At that time I was working at a government funded training centre with 16 to 18 year olds who had left mainstream school. I prepared them for work and also tutored them in Math and English, so they could sit their exams. Unsurprisingly, what my mother had told me really upset me and I lashed out at Sarah. This also ruined my relationship with my cousins Brad and Lucy, as they stuck by their mother and I became the enemy.

CHAPTER 16
BLOOD RELATIVES OR SELF-MADE FAMILIES?

During this time, I was looking for somewhere else to live. My mother had spoken to my cousin Charmaine and was trying to convince me to move in with her. I wasn't entirely sure I wanted to. It was quite far from work and I liked to keep myself separate from my family, as I was a very private person and did not tend to mix my personal life with them. Our family was like a gossip train; something would happen and within minutes it would be spread to everyone. I had kept things from my mother for years. I didn't want her to know anything about me. The idea of moving in with my cousin worried me that my private life would start to clash with my mother.

I did eventually agree to move in with my Charmaine, despite feeling pushed into it and just as I suspected a few weeks in, my mother started questioning me about my whereabouts and it all became overwhelming. There came a day when my mother told me that my Grandmother told her my Aunty Katrina; Charmaine's mother, had been talking badly about me and again I lashed out. I felt suffocated. For years now, I had been free of my mother's control and I suddenly felt like my actions and thoughts were being dictated by my mother again. It was too close to home.

An opportunity came for me to move closer to work. It was only two months since I had moved in with Charmaine and I was worried it wouldn't work out. It was such a big risk to move in with someone I hardly knew. *What would I do if it all went wrong?* I had always been a bit of a risk taker though, so I went with it and hoped for the best.

It did not take long for me to realise this had been the best risk I had ever taken. A few months in, and I already felt part of the family. Roe, the woman I was renting a room from was extremely warm and friendly. She had an aura that oozed safety. She is probably the most loving person I have ever met. When they say someone has a heart of gold, I think Roe was the inspiration for this. I opened up to her a lot about my mother, and for the first time in ages I felt like I belonged. Roe used to be a foster carer, so she knew exactly how to make you feel loved, when it had been so foreign to you. Despite how terrible my real family was, I had been blessed with such an amazing extended family with both Natalie and Roe.

I felt my mother grow more and more jealous of my relationship with Roe over the months. I had developed a very strong mother-daughter relationship with her. For years, I had longed for a relationship like this. In fact, I had prayed for it and spent my whole life dreaming what it would be like to have a mother that loved me, someone I could cry my eyes out to, go to advice for, or to just give me a hug when I was having a bad day. Everyone needs that mother's shoulder to cry on from time to time and I had finally found it in Roe.

Christmas was approaching and everyone was in a festive mood. It was the day of my work party and I had a doctor's appointment for some extremely bad headaches I had been getting that caused me to blackout. After explaining my symptoms to my GP, he advised me to go straight to the hospital. Shortly after they had taken some blood, I blacked out again. One minute, I was telling the nurse exactly what I had told my GP, the next thing I knew I was laying on the hospital floor with a load of nurses surrounding me. It was such a scary experience to go through, waking up feeling confused, not comprehending where I was and not seeing any familiar faces.

I had to stay in for a few hours after that for more tests. I asked my boss to ring my mother and let her know what had happened. My boss had driven me to the hospital, so knew what was going on. I was expecting my mother to come straight to the hospital, so that I wouldn't be there alone. I don't know why I expected such compassion from her. The only contact I received from my mother was a text message, asking why I had not told her I was unwell. I laughed to myself at the irony. Most mothers would not need to be told their child was unwell, as they would know through being present in their lives. While I lay in the hospital bed feeling sorry for myself, I received a call from Roe. She was in Australia, but still cared enough to call and make sure I was okay. She stayed on the phone with me for ages, reassuring me that everything would be okay and to keep her updated. Obviously, there was a huge time difference, so I told her to get some sleep and that I would call her when I had an update.

I rang my mother while I was waiting for my test results, to let her know that they were concerned that it was to do with my heart, as I have an irregular heartbeat. She started shouting, "Why did I have to find out about this from your boss? I don't need this stress today." Like I had planned this all, so that I could ruin my mother's day. I quickly brought the conversation to an end to avoid adding any extra stress to myself. Luckily, I got my results back and I was fine. I had a trapped nerve that was triggering the pains up my head, and causing the blackout headaches.

As Christmas day was approaching, my mother told me that my Aunties had been bad mouthing me again. I got really upset; she was constantly telling me the things that had been said about me. I got quite defensive, as I was fed up with her telling me the same old things. I asked her why my Aunties were always so comfortable to speak about me in this way, and why she never said anything to stop them. If anyone dared speak about my children the way my mother claimed they spoke about me, it would have been World War 3. Our ticking time bomb exploded because I had stood up to her, and she shouted back that she was going to tell them not to say things about me anymore. I would believe it when I saw it. Perhaps, they in fact weren't saying any of these things, and it was just my mother's way of causing a divide between us.

My Aunty Katrina was due to come round that evening and seeing as I would be at my mother's house at the time I was expecting her to bring it up with her, just like she had told me she would. I could not have predicted what actually happened. As my Aunt rang the buzzer, my mother asked me to go and sit in my sister's room until my Aunt left. I looked at her in disbelief. I told her I was not going to hide away, but she begged me to just do it. Before she could convince me, my Aunty had already been let in and they went straight into the kitchen, walking right passed me without saying a word.

My blood was boiling and I couldn't get over what had just happened. My mother had spent the best part of the day saying how she was going to tell my Aunt not to be disrespectful towards me, and that she was going to tell her a few home truths. Yet, now she was in the kitchen offering her tea and cake. Why did she even invite her over, knowing I was there and all of this was going on? It felt like one big mind game.

As a tear fell down my face, I decided I couldn't stay there and listen to my two-faced mother. I rang Natalie and she told me to go to her house. I left my mother's house without anyone even realising. About an hour later, my mother sent me a text message saying I was selfish and rude and that she wanted me to come and get the things I had left there. I waited for her to leave the next day before going round. Before I left, I took the Christmas present I had brought my mother from under the tree and hugged my sister goodbye.

When I got home it was cold and dark; no one had been in the house for days so the boiler had gone out. I sat down and put the TV on to find that it had been cut off due to the bill not being paid. Roe was in Australia, so she had forgotten to sort it out. All of a sudden, I burst into a flood of tears. Two days before Christmas, and I am sat there alone, with no heating and no TV.

I rang my cousin Lola and she told me to go to her house. While I was waiting for my cab, my mother called. I answered and she called me selfish, saying that I ruined Christmas for them. I screamed at her, "Like my Christmas isn't ruined?!" She asked me what I expected her to do, and I told her that instead of telling me what everyone was saying about me, why she doesn't either stop telling me what's being said or stand up for me. She screamed back, "I'll tell them all, I'll cut them all off. I hope you are happy now, because that's all that matters, isn't it? As long as Kylie is happy." Then she hung up.

All I wanted was for my mother to have my back for once. I was sick of her taunting me with what people had said about me, then ranting and raving about how she was going to pull them up about it, only for her to pretend nothing had happened when she saw them. Why would she want to continue to cause me so much pain and anger by telling me these things, if she wasn't going to do anything about it? For years, she had done this and sat back and watched while I lashed out at people. I was learning to manage these emotions and not lash out at what had been said, but rather to do everything in my power to prove everyone wrong. My mother, on the other hand, just seemed to keep breaking me down, piece by piece, waiting for me to flip and lash out at the world again. She thrived off me having drama with everyone. Not this time.

When she realised I wasn't going to back down on this occasion and that I would rather spend Christmas by myself than rise to her mind games, she rang me back. She told me that she had it out with my Aunty Sarah and that she missed me and wanted to sort things out between us. I was still confused at why my mother had spoken to Sarah and not Katrina, considering she was supposedly the one that had been saying things about me, but it was a start. My mother said that she was meeting Sarah for lunch the next day; Christmas Eve, and that Sarah wanted me to meet them as well. I agreed and went to meet them.

When I arrived, things were awkward. Sarah and I just stood there and said hello to each other until my mother turned round and said "Kylie meet Sarah, Sarah meet Kylie." It still felt a bit odd. Sarah seemed shocked to see me, despite her supposedly suggesting this meet, but the tension eased up and it got easier. Over time, I managed to restore a relationship with my Aunty Sarah and my cousins.

2013 turned out to be a pretty normal year. My mother and I seemed to be building a relationship like we had never had before. She would confide in me a lot about Kiara and Kevin. They were both teenagers now. My mother would ring me complaining about how little they did around the house. It almost felt nice to not be the scapegoat for once. She would tell me how selfish they both were and how Kevin didn't do anything except things for himself.

She built up this image of a boy who wanted everything, but did nothing to earn it. It annoyed me that he was so ungrateful and he was always so dismissive of me whenever I went over. The stories my mother was telling me about him were starting to get my back up. One day, I was staying over at my mother's house when Kevin started arguing with Kiara and me about watching a movie in the room he was in. By this point, I'd had enough of his attitude and ended up getting into a massive argument with him. We ended up not talking for the rest of the year. If I went to my mother's, we would walk past each other as if the other did not even exist. My mother never did anything to resolve the issue. I'd had enough conflict with my mother over time though, so I just let it be. Things between my mother and I continued to be calm. Every time I came to visit, my mother waited on me hand and foot, which was new to me, yet it started to cause conflict between Kiara and I.

CHAPTER 17
SOMETHING'S BREWING

Towards the end of this normal feeling year, my mother started to act strange. She was always in her bed playing on her phone. She stopped spending time with me when I went to visit. Kane would just be alone in the living room watching TV. I worried. I wondered if my mother was suffering from depression. I visited more often than usual, both to spend time with Kane and to ensure my mother was okay. As Christmas was approaching, Kevin and I were still not talking. My mother said that she was not going to have such an atmosphere between us over Christmas dinner, so I told her I would be going to Natalie's for Christmas dinner anyway. I thought she would react to this, but she didn't care.

I started 2014 promising myself this was going to be the best year by far. I was optimistic. The last year felt like I had made progress with my mother for the first time in my life; little did I know this was about to become the worst year of my life.

My mother was still being strange. I would talk to her, but she wasn't listening. Always on her phone, smiling and laughing. It was a rare occasion to see my mother smile. She didn't even crack a smile on her wedding day, so I was suspicious of her behaviour. She started wearing make-up, and even drinking quite a bit. She had always judged us if we went out and had more than a few drinks. My whole life the woman that had hardly ever drunk, had numerous hangovers in the same month. *Was she having a mid-life crisis?*

Kiara and I had grown closer. Kiara confessed the reason she would get so annoyed with me when my mother had been doing everything for me, was due to the way my mother would regularly complain about me when I wasn't around. Kiara was older, so she understood my relationship with my mother better. It was actually nice to have someone to speak to that understood. I told Kiara stories about my time growing up, as I could relate to what she was starting to experience with my mother and offer advice. Kiara could not believe some of the things I was telling her, it was then and there that we both realised our mother had been lying to us and twisting the truth for years. Telling us her own versions of events to cause conflicts between us. It suddenly made sense to me why Kevin had been acting that way; my mother had played us both against each other. I would fix this, but I had to focus on one thing at a time.

I could see how stressed Kiara was over the way things were at home. I never told her of my suspicions as that would just add to her stress. If my mother was not having a mid-life crisis, then she was having an affair. A few weeks after Kiara and I had compared stories, Kiara sent me a message, "Mum is going out this weekend with Aunty Sarah."

I knew this was odd, and Kiara did too. My mother never went anywhere; with her recent strange behaviour this rang massive alarm bells. I told Kiara I would sort this out. Mike had also started to notice the change in my mother, and was confiding in Kiara a lot. Having to deal with her father crying to her was too much for her to deal with. She was still so young, not even 18 years old. I had to protect her, my baby sister. I never wanted her to feel the pain I had felt growing up. That was why I agreed to sort things out.

I messaged Aunty Sarah and I asked her if she was free that weekend. She told me she was not and that she was going wedding dress shopping with her friend. My mother's plans then suddenly changed. She told Kiara that Sarah had cancelled on her and that she was going to go for dinner with the neighbour Sana. This still did not sit right with either Kiara or me. For years, all my mother had done was complain about Sana and how she did not like her, yet suddenly they were going out for dinner.

I suspected Kiara had started to get the same suspicions as me, I was proven correct when she rang me the next morning. The phone call woke me up and I answered in a panic, as Kiara never rung me. She always texted, because we couldn't let my mother know we had a relationship, otherwise she would try to destroy it. I think she could hear the worry in my voice, so she quickly blurted out "Mum never came home last night."

Mike had waited up until 3am, but never heard from her. He was too scared to ring her, as he said she would just start shouting at him for checking up on her; how ridiculous that my mother has made someone too scared to be concerned for her wellbeing. It was now 10am; my mother being hurt or in danger hadn't even crossed my mind, as I somehow knew this day was coming. I told Kiara not to worry and that I was on my way. By the time I got there, my mother was home. She had just got out of the shower when I arrived, and she asked me what I was doing there. She couldn't even look at me and was rushing around saying she needed to leave. My mother had never arrived anywhere on time; so this sudden urgency to leave had guilt all over it.

I started to question her about her evening, ignoring her strange behaviour.

"How was last night?"

She wouldn't look at me. "Last night?"

"Didn't you go out with Sarah," I questioned, acting dumb and pretending that I did not know her plans had changed.

She got defensive and said that she had been out with Sana, as Sarah had let her down and they just went to get some food. She did not mention that she stayed out, and before I could ask her anything else, she called for Mike and told him they were going. Kiara came out of her room once my mother had left and for the first time ever I heard her say it.

"I think Mum is having an affair."

I could see the upset in her eyes when I responded that I had thought so for a while. I couldn't see my sister so stressed out; all she was doing was worrying about this. We needed to know the truth. I grabbed my mother's laptop and opened up her internet. The first thing we saw was a booking for a hotel room. I looked at Kiara and she burst into tears. I comforted her and told her I would sort this out, talk to our mother, and get her to do the right thing. If she didn't want to be with Mike all she had to do was tell him; all these lies were just going to destroy so many people. We opened her Facebook to try and find out who this guy was. She had messages with Mike's best friend's wife; laughing about what an idiot Mike was, saying that she was going to leave him and go off with this new guy. The wife was also complaining about how her husband had not come home the night before. Kiara and I looked at each other in horror. Our mother was having an affair with Mike's best friend, Sean - and had been confiding in his wife! My mother was more twisted than I thought.

I couldn't stay there any longer. I couldn't be there when my mother got back. Kiara begged me not to say anything until her exams were over. She knew what would unfold if this came out before. We were in the month of January, her last exam was in June. I wasn't sure I would be able to put on this pretence for that long, but I promised I wouldn't say anything until she was ready. I just wanted to take all her stresses away, deep down I knew I couldn't. I was angry that I couldn't confront my mother about it, but I had to bite my tongue. All I did was message her and ask her if I could have the money she owed me. I made out that I needed it, but the truth was I was annoyed that she was using her money on hotels, when she had said she couldn't afford to give me the money she owed me.

CHAPTER 18
THE AFFAIR

The next day Kiara messaged me saying she couldn't do this another day longer, as she couldn't sit there and watch her father breaking down, he was telling her that my mother said she was leaving, as she did not love him anymore. Kiara couldn't lie to him when she knew the truth. I told her I would sort it out that day. I texted my mother asking if she wanted to meet me for a drink after work, but she replied back saying she was busy. I told her that I needed to talk to her about something and she asked me what it was. *Why did she always have to be so complicated and difficult.* I told her I needed to speak to her face to face, she asked me why. Again, I told her I needed to talk to her face to face and that if she wasn't willing to, then I wasn't willing to tell her what it was about; she just said okay.

I could not believe what had just happened. I could have needed to talk to her about anything. I could have been in trouble, I could have needed her help. Then I realised, she knew that I knew. She was avoiding me, cutting me off so she wouldn't have to face the truth. I grew angry. More so that I couldn't just have a normal relationship, where I could ask my mother to meet me and she just would, no questions asked. She wouldn't answer my calls and she wouldn't meet me so I had to have this entire discussion, via text message:

Me: *Mum, we really need to talk. I'm worried about you and I'm worried about the kids. Please just come and meet me.*

Mother: *Talk about what? Why are you worried about me for? Will have your money for you tomorrow.*

Me: *Thanks. Are you going to meet me for that chat then? Let me know what time, as I am teaching.*

Mother: *Look, if you can't tell me then I don't want to know.*

Me: *Can't a daughter just want to talk to her mother without all these questions?*

Mother: *Really?*

Me: *Yes really.*

She didn't reply after this. And she never turned up to bring me my money either. I was getting really annoyed with the way she always avoided things. I messaged her saying "I thought you were coming today?" She ignored it.

Kiara said things were really bad at home. Mike was pleading with her to stay with him, blaming himself for her not loving him anymore. Trying to figure out what he had done wrong. This was not going to go away. And she wasn't going to shut me out again. My whole life I had just kept my mouth shut, to prevent really telling her what I had thought, because I was too scared to confront her, but I wasn't scared of her anymore. Just like when I had written that letter and she ignored it. This was not going away this time. I wasn't going to be silenced. I composed a message that I knew was about to open a can of worms but I was ready for it...

Me: *You continuing to ignore me is not going to make me disappear. It is also not going to excuse the fact that I know you are having an affair. Don't try and deny it because I have the proof. If you can be caught out by me it's only a matter of time before the rest of your children clock on. And just like you lost the respect you had from me, you will lose it from them. You don't deserve someone like Mike and if you want to destroy this family then just leave by yourself, then you can do whatever you want. Let's hope Sean will be there for you then! I also want my money by the end of the week.*

Mother: *I'm not ignoring you. You respect me? Ha! Like you or anyone in this house has any for me. I'll just get on with my own thing and f**k the rest of you. How dare you talk to me like this? You think I'm one of your kids? I'm sick of the way everyone talks to me and treats me! This family was f**ked up a long time ago. And that's you isn't it, you never give you only take.*

Me: *You had respect, but you never look closer to home. You always want to blame us. You need to look at your own behaviours. We are the products of what you produced, so you're the one that messed up not us. And after years of your bulls**t behaviour, I'm done. I'm not all about taking, not at all, but you only ever see the bad in us. You better tell Mike about your affair. If you don't I will.*

Mother: *You do that but don't come back to this house. My bulls**t behaviour! Really? Ok*

Me: *Just know that when the rest of your kids leave you like I have it's all on you!*

Mother: *Leave like you have? Really? You left years ago, didn't you? Has never been the same*

Me: *And why do you think I left?*

Mother: *Go on tell me. Think it was the way Mike treated you. If I'm right.*

Me: *Do I really have to spell it out? You were the one that made me leave! You were that one that packed my stuff! You were the one that dismantled my bed! You always have to pass the blame!*

Mother: *Erm, hello! Really? Ok. You better have a long think about that now.*

Me: *You're the one that needs to think. Stop blaming your children and take some responsibility for once.*

Mother: *You went off to university and said you were not coming back, because of the fight you had with Mike. I didn't pack your stuff.*

Me: *You did pack my stuff. I moved out in second year. Why? Because of you! And what did you threaten to do when I told you? You threatened to get rid of Kane. You don't even realise the emotional abuse we have all put up with from you!*

Mother: *Emotional abuse? Haha! Really? Ok*

Me: *You never see when you are in the wrong.*

Mother: *No I never do. I'm the one always in the wrong. Well you lot will be better off without me in your lives if I have f**ked you all up.*

Me: *I thought you would have learnt from your mistakes that you made with me.*

Mother: *Mistakes I made with you! Haha. I did my very best for all of you!*

Me: *Don't be surprised when you start getting déjà vu*

Mother: *Really?*

Me: *You know what you're never going to see the error in your ways. So, I'm not getting into this. Just make sure you tell Mike the truth.*

Mother: *You're the one that started this.*

Me: *So you better end it*

Mother: *Goodbye*

Me: *Just make sure you tell him*

Mother: *Because you would be happy to. You're crazy. Don't tell me what to do.*

Me: *Don't forget to give me my money. Then me and you are done*

    My mother then sent me a picture of the letter I had written her, before I went to housesit after Mike and I had the fight where he almost hit me.

Mother: *So what's this all about? Think he's messed up your head. That's why you left.*

Me: *You need to remember what happened after that. You're the one that messed up my head. That one occasion six years ago! What about everything in between?*

Mother: *Yeah ok, just like my sisters hey? Well you hate them so you must hate me too. Well I've known this for years. Don't come back to this house again do you hear me. And don't think you will see Kane ever again*

Me: *Ohhh, I was waiting for that! Always play him as a weapon. Well you're wrong mother. I will see him.*

Mother: *No I don't. And you won't see him, not if I can help it. I'm going to keep him well away from you with your f**ked up head.*

Me: *What, so you can mess him up too? He needs to be kept away from you! You're pathetic*

Mother: *Yeah, a bit like you really. Telling me to tell Mike. Who the hell are you to tell me what to do?*

Me: *Well, I tried to talk to you about this like adults the other day, but you didn't want to hear it*

Mother: *You wouldn't tell me*

Me: *Like I said I wanted to do this like adults and talk to you reasonably face to face*

Mother: *You know you lot are always telling me what to do.*

I didn't bother responding after that; this would keep going back and forth otherwise. This was the final straw for me. There was no going back from this. I officially had no ounce of love left for my mother. I hated her. She still wasn't taking responsibility for any of this and was trying to turn it all around on me.

The next day she messaged me.

"I've told him now fuck off and leave us alone. I hope you are happy in your sad little life. He doesn't want to talk to you, he thinks you're sick. You have upset everyone once again."

I was fuming! I've upset everyone?! My mother has had an affair and I have upset everyone!? She always had to find a way to make everything my fault. I knew she was lying about what she had told Mike, there was no way he would respond like that towards me over my mother having an affair. She was gaslighting me to stay away from Mike. She didn't want him knowing the real truth.

A few days after all of this, Mike called me and asked if we could meet up. I agreed to meet him in a café not far from where we both lived. He turned up with Kiara. Mike looked a mess, he had aged ten years in the space of two days and his eyes had sunken into his face. He almost looked as if his soul had left his body. He sat down and just looked at me trembling. He asked me what was going on, and said that my mother had told him she was seeing someone, but that it was over now. He had his head hung the whole time, but he suddenly looked up and looked me in the eyes. His eyes were bloodshot, he stuttered on his words.

"Why is your mother not talking to you? I know there is more to this than she has told me. You know who it is, don't you?"

I told him I would not tell him, but that I also would not lie to him if anything he wanted to ask me. He asked if it was someone he knew.

"Yes." I replied.

He clasped his hands around his mouth pulling his eyes down as he did, trying to figure out who it could be. He was reeling off names of people he thought it could be, when Kiara stopped him.

"It's Sean."

He looked at us both in disbelief, tears pouring down his face as he mouthed, "Sean." Too shocked to get any words out at first, he then started shouting, "How could he do this to me? I confided in him!" He asked how we knew for sure it was Sean, we told him about what we had seen on my mother's laptop. I stayed with them until I knew Mike was going to be okay and not do anything stupid. I begged him to not let my mother find out that Kiara knew, as I did not want her to treat her the way she had been treating me. He said he was not going to say anything for a while. He wanted to see if she confessed herself. He pleaded with Kiara and I not to hate him if he left her; we reassured him that this would never happen. Before he left, I asked him for one thing and one thing only.

"Please make sure I get to see Kane!"

For the next few days, I had to put up with Mike breaking down to me multiple times a day. He came to my house in the evenings - crying his eyes out. He called me in the mornings before I started work - crying down the phone from his car. He was a nervous wreck.

He continued to pretend that he didn't know who my mother was having the affair with. He wanted to see if it really was over. I told him it was a bad idea to carry on this way, as I was worried he would explode and do something stupid. However, he insisted and to be honest I really didn't care anymore. I just wanted to be able to see Kane. Mike asked me if I would message Sean's wife and tell her that while she was helping my mother cover up her affair, my mother was actually taking her for a fool, and she was having the affair with her husband. I told him that I didn't think it was a good idea, but he pleaded with me, so I said I would message her if he really thought that was the right thing to do.

He also asked me if I could call his other friends, explaining to them what was going on. He said they had been trying to get in contact with him, but he couldn't speak to them as my mother was around. Again, I didn't really want to get involved, but I did tell him I would be there for him, so if this is what he felt he needed then, so be it. I called his friend Mitchel and filled him in on everything. After speaking with him for twenty minutes, Mitchel said:

"You're a really lovely girl. You're not the horrible ogre your mother makes you out to be."

I sat there for a second shocked, I had no idea who this man was, yet my mother had clearly been feeding him made up stories about me over the years. Who does that? In that moment I realised my mother was messier than I thought. I told Mitchel I had to go, and that he should message Mike should he have any other questions. I was over it.

When I next spoke to Mike, I told him I wasn't doing any more of his dirty work. I didn't need to be hearing what my mother had been saying about me from strangers. It was almost as if he wanted to stir the pot even more. He ignored what I was saying, and went on to tell me that my mother had been bad mouthing me to my childhood friend's mother too. Saying things like "she goes on all these holidays, but doesn't have a pot to piss in." *Why was he telling me this?* I had just told him how I couldn't hear all this negativity anymore, and he continued to tell me more things that she had been saying about me.

I went home from work that day feeling emotionally exhausted after a week of consoling Mike, and being there for him day and night, only to have all the bullshit turned on me. Roe saw me walk through the door and instantly knew something was up. I told her what had happened, and I broke down, I was sick of being the adult in this situation. Why was I having to parent my "parents." Just as we were about to sit down to eat dinner, the doorbell went.

Roe went to answer the door, it was Mike. He was carrying a box of things with him. As he gave them to me, I opened the box to realise they were my baby keepsakes, things like the hospital gown I wore when I was born and my first baby comforter. When Roe saw what was in the box and the look on my face, she flipped. Now, as I already mentioned, Roe has one of the purest, kindest hearts you will ever come across, but you DO NOT want to cross her if you hurt someone she cares about. She turned to Mike, I thought she was about to hit him, she started marching him towards the front door.

"I've had to sit here every night and watch you cry on that poor girl's shoulder, and for what?!? For you to bring this box here, like she can just be chucked to the curb. You need to man up and grow some fucking balls, get out of my house and don't you dare step foot on my doorstep again."

As soon as she slammed the door behind him I burst into tears, how had all of this turned me to the villain? My mother has an affair, I try to talk to her about it, and suddenly I am shunned by everyone. I honestly thank my lucky stars for Roe, because I couldn't have got through all of this without her. I couldn't be strong in this situation but she kept me strong.

The next day, I received a call from my Grandmother. She started scolding me down the phone, asking me why I had been so rude and disrespectful to my mother. I stopped her, expressing that I didn't know what my mother had told her, but that I was going to tell her the truth. I told her the real reason why my mother and I had fallen out. My Grandmother apologised. She didn't understand why my mother would make up lies about me. I could, she was doing everything in her power to try and get a reaction out of me, however because that wasn't working, she had to go out and paint a picture of me to everyone else - before I got there with the truth, in the hope that everyone would turn on me and I wouldn't have a chance to tell them. More fool my mother, I had no intention of telling my Grandmother what had happened, she didn't need to be involved or have any stress worrying about any of us. Yet, I couldn't sit back and let her think such terrible things of me, in order to protect my mother, so I told her everything.

CHAPTER 19
SO, THIS IS WHAT HEARTBREAK FEELS LIKE?

The next few months were extremely difficult. I had been cut deep into my soul. I didn't know if I would ever see Kane again, I had never felt pain like this. I felt empty, everything was dark and heavy. I can truly say I've seen rock bottom. I cried myself to sleep every night, I cried at work, in the shower, in the supermarket, making dinner. Everything was triggering me. I was so worried that Kane would think I had abandoned him because I didn't love him. I begged my sister to let him know I cared about him, but at the same time, I appreciated this was difficult for her. She was still a child herself, but it was my only option.

Kane was 5 years old at the time, yet he knew, and it hurt me even more to know how much understanding he had over the situation. Kiara was filming him messing around one day, when he turned to her and said, "Mummy doesn't like Ky Ky, she told me." My sister was in shock, but she sent it to me and strangely it reassured me. He knew that I wasn't around because of her. He would secretly send me messages from Kiara's phone. They would only be a load of emojis, but I knew he had carefully selected each one that he did send and they made me smile. He would send me little voice notes too. The sound of his sweet innocent voice used to melt my heart, I couldn't give up on him, but at the same time I wasn't sure I was strong enough to fight to see him either.

Eventually, my mother found out about our messages and went ballistic. My sister got into a lot of trouble, and she was too scared to let him message me anymore. I was back to feeling lost without that little form of communication with him.

All I could think about was Kane, how was I going to stay in his life, hoping he wouldn't have to experience an upbringing like mine. I went to see a solicitor, to find out if I had any rights to gaining access to him. This was a waste of time however, as they told me it would cost me thousands of pounds to take to court, to fight a battle I wouldn't win.

I couldn't let Kane think I didn't care. After months of not seeing him, on his 6th birthday, I decided to just turn up at my mother's house. What was the worst that could happen? I was already at an all-time low. I knocked on the door, I could hear Mike, in his worst discreet voice ever calling to my mother saying "It's Kylie." My mother answered and she did not look impressed, Kane came running around the corner, as soon as he saw me his face lit up and he shouted "Ky Ky!"

"I just came to drop off Kane's present," I stated.

My mother looked at Kane, who was now grinning from ear to ear, as she reluctantly told me to come in. Kane and I were both ecstatic. He was so excited showing me everything he got for his birthday. He asked me if I would play Monopoly with him. I was letting him win; he's always hated losing. Yet, this time he didn't seem to want to win. He kept giving me his money when I was close to losing, when I asked him why he was doing that he said, "If it's not game over then you won't have to go home." I wanted to cry. It's his 6th birthday he shouldn't be worrying about these things.

When it was time for me to leave, Kane was really upset. I gave him a big hug and told him if it is a while until we see each other again, to remember how much I loved him. Although I was happy that I was able to spend his birthday with him, I still couldn't help feeling heavy-hearted, because I didn't know if there would be a time I could see him again. So, I walked home in tears, hoping this would not be the end.

CHAPTER 20
DEEPENING THE WOUNDS OF A BROKEN HEART

Another four weeks went by without me seeing Kane. I was packing to leave for the airport, as I was flying out to Dubai for my birthday with Natalie. I had just about finished with my packing when my phone rang. It was Kiara. I instantly thought something was wrong - as you know she didn't usually call me. I answered and she sounded upset.

"What's up," I asked.

"Nanny died," I heard back.

Everything around me went blurry and I dropped to my knees. It felt like I was in slow motion and all the sounds around me had been muted. Kiara was talking, but I couldn't tell you what she was saying. I let out a bloodcurdling scream, and burst into tears. The 29th of April 2014, the day my first ever mother figure was ripped out of my life. *She couldn't be gone.* Please tell me this is an awful nightmare and I'm about to wake up!

I thought I had already hit rock bottom. Turns out there was a basement that I didn't know about. I couldn't accept that she was gone. I called her phone, praying she would answer. It rang out to her voicemail, I cried even harder when I heard her voice. I must have called back over 100 times, just to hear her voice on the voicemail.

I called Natalie and told her what had happened. She immediately suggested we cancel the holiday. I thought about it for a minute and told her I still wanted to go. My grandmother loved that I was so well-travelled, she would want me to go. Besides, what else was I meant to do, stay here with my unsupportive mother, who would no doubt make me feel worse? Despite the fact that my mother and I were not talking, I still couldn't stop thinking about her. She had just lost her mother. I have been grieving my own mother for the last seven years. So, I thought I knew how she was feeling.

As I sat there waiting for Natalie to come and collect me for the airport, I pondered on why my mother didn't call me herself to tell me. Perhaps she was too upset, but Kiara was 18 years old, she shouldn't have been the one that had to tell me. I decided I was going to message my mother and see how she was.

I started typing, "Are you okay?" I hovered over the send button for a while. Was this the right thing to do? She's grieving too, I told myself. So I pressed the button. She responded back straight away saying, "Yeah, you?"

I regretted my decision instantly. Why did I think I would get some emotion from this woman? I had opened a can of worms and I knew this day was going to come back to bite me. I didn't reply, by the time I arrived at the airport I received even more messages from her, telling me that all the sisters were already arguing and she was bitching about them all. I was so glad I hadn't decided to stay. That was the confirmation I needed to get on that plane.

We had a night flight, so by the time we took off everyone had fallen asleep. I stayed awake the whole flight, luckily it was pretty empty, so I had a row that was empty and laid across the seats. I covered my head with a blanket and cried the majority of the flight. The flight attendant had noticed and asked me if I was okay, I told her about my Grandmother and every so often she would come and check on me, bringing me tea and other snacks. It was actually quite nice to be disconnected from the world.

I thought about all the wonderful memories I had with my Grandmother, we lived with her until I was 5 years old, so we had a special bond. I saw a side to her I don't think many did, a silly side. My mother used to be away a lot over the weekends, and my Grandmother and I would have breakfast in bed together. She would tell me stories and do silly voices. We would laugh so much. I wished I had made more time for her, I would call her every week and chat for hours, but I'd wished I visited more. I reminisced on all those phone calls, all our chats about the Kardashians, and her favourite Bollywood movies. I know she cherished those calls. I would do anything to have just one more of them. To hear her say, "*I love you*" just one last time. I still have her number saved in my phone to this day. I can't bring myself to delete it. I sometimes pick up the phone and go to call her and then I remember, she's gone.

We arrived in Dubai and I didn't have any more messages from my mother. I wanted to just try and enjoy this break away from reality, for my Grandmother, I knew she would be looking down on me. The next morning I woke up and saw I had 5 messages from my mother. It was my birthday, so I thought to myself *maybe she does care.*

I opened them up to see the first message telling me that my Grandmother's autopsy would be in 4 days' time, and the rest of the messages were about the arguments between the sisters again. Why did I think she would acknowledge my birthday, why would she message me this information on my birthday? I didn't reply to her until I returned back to the UK. I told her my messages were not sending because my roaming wasn't working. I couldn't deal with her getting into my head while I was on this trip. I needed to process my Grandmother's death.

When I returned from Dubai, everything was different. It was almost like the last four months had never happened. My mother called me to ask me if I had a nice time and asked me if I wanted to come over. I was so confused; but then, my mother did have a habit of brushing things under the carpet and pretending like nothing had happened. There would never be any apology or accountability from her. It would just disappear. As weird as it was, I went with it. I hadn't been able to see Kane, so I decided to make the most of it while I could. I already knew nothing lasted forever with this woman.

CHAPTER 21
CAN I MEND THEIR HEARTS?

I was hanging out with Kane more and more. My mother messaged me a lot, trying to make plans for me to meet her to go shopping with her and Kane, I didn't want to spend time with her though. I hated her, so I offered to watch Kane while she went shopping. I loved being able to have this time with him, he wasn't the same little boy he used to be though. I noticed that sadness in his eyes, the same sadness I had from when I was a child. The once funny, extroverted little boy had now become a nervous, emotional child, with so much worry on his shoulders. He was also having a lot of panic attacks at the time, my mother was trying to put it down to my Grandmother's passing, however I knew they were a result of the frosty atmosphere in the house since the affair. Everyone was walking around on eggshells, whilst my mother swanned around like she was invincible. It infuriated me how she couldn't see how much damage she had caused and was still causing.

One evening, I was sat speaking with my sister waiting for Kane to get out of the bath when I heard him screaming, I rushed to the bathroom as the screams sounded like someone was trying to drown him. My mother was only trying to wash his hair, but the cries had so much pain in them. He started to have a panic attack and was shouting "I'm sorry" over and over again. It was heart-breaking to watch him in this state. I told my mother I would get him ready for bed, so that I could speak to him. We played with his teddies, while he was getting into his pyjamas. He loved the voices I made for them. To hear his little innocent laugh was something I had missed so much.

"What makes you happy Kane?" I asked him, now he seemed in better spirits.

"Spending time with you," he replied instantly. He had always been a little cutie and knew how to pull on those heart strings.

"That makes me happy too, and what makes you sad?"

He hung his head as his tone changed and he told me, "It makes me sad when mummy and daddy shout at each other, and when mummy is mad at you."

I wanted to cry and give him the biggest hug, but I needed to be strong and show him I was there for him. I never had anyone to talk to as a child, no one that I could trust, so I needed to try and be that person for him.

"Why were you saying sorry when you were crying?" I asked him.

"Because that is what my daddy says when he cries," he replied as he picked up his toys for me to play.

I wanted to leave his bedroom and smash my mother and Mike's heads together. Why could they not see that the selfishness of them airing their dramas in front of anyone and everyone was damaging their children? I told my mother what Kane had said, but she still excused the panic attacks and said they were a result of losing my Grandmother. She was never going to see the errors in her ways. I just had to continue to be there as much as I could for my siblings.

This was difficult for me though, as it felt as though my mother thought I was there for her. I would get messages from her saying things like "Mike is playing up" and one day, she even told me that he had started cutting himself as she discovered the cuts all over his arms. *What did she want me to do with this information?* They were both as toxic as each other and I was over their drama. No one was doing anything about Kane's panic attacks or even noticed the anxiety it was causing Kiara and Kevin. I was not about to start counselling these so-called adults again. My siblings were my only concern.

A few weeks later, I was at home cooking my dinner, when Kiara called me, as always when she called I instantly knew something was up. I answered the phone, I could barely understand what she was saying. She was hyperventilating so much all I managed to catch was "chasing my dad… I have no shoes on… he ran out the house… I had to take a knife off him."

I told her I was on my way, I had no idea where they were but my mother's house was just under 2 miles away from mine. I turned the stove off and ran. I ran all the way there without stopping. I'm not the best runner, as I have asthma and always get out of breath, but something gave me the power that day to run, I could hardly breathe and my shins felt like my bones were about to snap out of my legs, but I made it. As soon as I arrived at my mother's house I saw Mike. He was crying so much, he had snot running out of his nose mixed in with his tears. He looked a wreck. He came walking towards me, holding his arms out for me to hug him. I pushed him out of the way.

"I am not here for you and your foolishness, I am here to make sure my sister is okay."

He pleaded with me, telling me he was sorry and how much he was hurting.

I screamed back at him saying "What, so that makes it okay for you to walk into my mother's room with a knife?!"

He stopped me and cried back, "It wasn't for her, it was for me."

This made me even angrier. He was so wrapped up in trying to get my mother's attention, he was causing more trauma to my siblings.

"So you were just going to kill yourself while your 6-year-old son was in the bath and your other two children are studying for their A-Level exams? Which they have tomorrow, by the way!"

He continued to cry as he responded how sorry he was, and that he just wanted to die. I was so angry - they never considered our feelings. I snarled back at him, "Go and jump off a bridge then." And then I pushed past to go and check on my siblings.

Mike remained outside, causing a scene. You could tell he was crying out for attention, and just needed someone to grab him and tell him everything was going to be okay. My mother had broken him, but I just couldn't show any empathy towards him. Look what had happened last time I was there for him! He threw me to the side as soon as he had my mother's attention back, and I was the one left crying alone. He wasn't consoling me. Had he even thought about our pain? Or how we were coping? Once I was sure my siblings were all okay, I went back outside. My mother had called Mike's friend to come and speak to him, because she said she was also over knowing what to do with him. Ironic, really, considering that she was the one that had caused all of this!

I sat outside with them as I listened to his friend telling him everything I had been thinking. Telling him he had to put the children first, and stop having these breakdowns in front of them. Telling him that he needed to go and see a councillor, suggesting perhaps him and my mother go together. She quickly shut that one down though, saying she didn't have a problem, he was the one with the problem. This was just typical of my mother - she could never accept her wrongs.

Mike continued to pour his heart out, then he started to express how he was struggling dealing with the loss of my Grandmother; *was he being serious?!* A rage built inside me, he started saying how he couldn't believe she was gone, and he was talking about when they went to clear her house, he had picked up the shoe she must have been wearing before she was found and maggots fell out of it. If I could have pushed him off a bridge there and then I would have. *How dare he!* How dare he sit there and talk about my Grandmother like this? First of all, they weren't even close. Secondly, did I really need to have the same image he claims to be struggling with, and know that my Grandmother was left there, helpless for days before she was found?

This was my Grandmother, she was my blood and I loved her so much. Yet, he thought he had the right to go around breaking down and causing a scene in her name. I screamed out, "How do you think I feel? I lost MY Grandmother, I am grieving too! Yet, here I am picking up the pieces for you again." I left after that, I couldn't continue to listen to this pity party he was throwing. I knew this was all a way to get attention from my mother, as he was still pussyfooting around her after the affair.

CHAPTER 22
GOODBYE MY FIRST MOTHER FIGURE

We waited for what seemed like forever for my Grandmother's funeral. It had been delayed a whole month after her death, as this was when it was most convenient for my mother. This caused conflict between my mother and her sisters, but my mother always got what she wanted. The day finally came for us to say goodbye, it was just as hard as the day I heard she was gone.

On the way to the chapel, I was in the car with my Aunty Sarah and Lucy. My mother had been awful to Sarah since my Grandmother passed away, so I wanted to keep close to her, as I knew what it was like to be on the receiving end of my mother's wrath. Sarah had wanted her best friend to come to the funeral to support her, but my mother said no one other than family was allowed. Yet, as we drove up to the chapel we saw Mike's father and brothers standing outside.

We all looked at each other in disbelief. Sarah was livid, they had never even met my Grandmother and they didn't speak to my mother, so, why had they been allowed to come but Sarah's best friend couldn't? Sarah wanted to confront my mother, but I told her it wasn't worth it. We sat separately from everyone else in the chapel. I squeezed Lucy's hand the whole time. I was shaking so much, and I was due to head to the altar to speak, as I had prepared a poem for my Grandmother. I headed up, took a deep breath and froze. I tried so hard to get my words out, but nothing was coming.

I hung my head low, tears pouring down my face for what felt like an eternity. *Why was no one coming to help me?* I decided to look up and find Kane, as I knew seeing his face would give me strength. As I looked up, I suddenly locked eyes with my mother instead. I will never forget the way she was glaring at me. Her eyes were fixated on me, cutting like daggers deep into my soul. There was so much hate! It was as though I had been the one that had killed my Grandmother. The sight of her made it even harder for me to say anything, eventually my cousin Charmaine came up and read the poem for me.

After the service was finished, Kiara and I went to say our final goodbyes and went to stand by my Grandmother's coffin before she was cremated. Her coffin had been wrapped with an image of the beach. She moved to the seaside when I was 8 years old and she loved it there. We held each other, as we cried our hearts out. I felt empty inside. I was so weak, my legs felt like they were about to break. I just needed someone to hug me and take me away. I saw my mother walking over to us and, for a second, I thought she was about to comfort us, for the first time in her life. Instead, she sniffled a bit and squeezed out a few crocodile tears, before Mike came over to her and wrapped his arm around her. They walked out, leaving Kiara and I breaking down, eventually, Kevin came and walked us to the car to head to the wake.

The wake couldn't have been more uncomfortable. My mother spent the whole time with that same neurotic look on her face. She didn't take her eyes off me, continuing those daggers I was getting from her in the chapel. Everyone kept asking me why my mother was behaving in such a way towards me. This was the first time she had ever shown her true colours towards me in public. There was a darkness around her, it scared me. I had never felt the hate from my mother like this before - yes she had emotionally abused me my entire life, but this felt different. The way she was looking at me that day is still something that haunts me now. I finally understood the saying "if looks could kill." She eventually left, and the day became a lot lighter. I was able to share stories about my Grandmother, with other members of the family who I didn't see often.

I've never really gotten over losing her. Every year approaching my birthday I get extremely sad. I don't think I will ever be truly happy on this day again. Maybe because I am now an adult dealing with the grief, but this pain felt different to when my Aunty Angela and Granddad passed away. I would give anything to have just one more day with her.

CHAPTER 23
MY PRISON SENTENCE

Despite the hate my mother was showing me at the funeral, the following day she messaged me like nothing had ever happened. She asked if I wanted to go to the park with Kane and her. I was starting to wonder if she was bipolar. Her moods were so up and down. I was still cautious of her behaviour though, so I kept things very limited after the funeral. Most of my replies to her messages would be simple one word answers, never giving her too much. I still had very strong feelings of hate towards her, but for the sake of seeing Kane, I couldn't let her know. I called this time of my life my 'Prison Sentence,' just biding my time until I was free. The amount of times I would be sat there imagining smashing my mother's face off a brick wall was quite scary. I had to be on my best behaviour if I was going to get through this prison sentence. She was making me become as bitter as she was. It was terrifying how much anger this woman made me feel.

Whenever anything would happen that could trigger an argument, I wrote it down. Each day got harder and harder to pretend, but documenting everything to build my case against cutting ties from her helped a great amount. There was also something quite healing about getting everything out of my system and writing it down.

The summer after my Grandmother's death, my mother was housesitting for a friend of mine. I found this particularly weird. She had always kept my friends close to her, not my closest friends, as she knew she couldn't put on a front with them, yet the friends who wouldn't have known the full extent of my mother's madness, she showed a great interest in them. Since her being out of the house was an extremely rare occasion, I decided I would stay at her house, so I could hang out with Kiara.

It was nice to be able to discuss how we were feeling about my mother, without worrying if listening ears were close by. It was also nice to spend time with Kiara and not have to hide that we had a relationship with each other. I had recently asked my mother for my birth certificate, yet she swore blind she did not have it and had already given it to me. I know for a fact I gave it to her when I moved house, so that she could keep it safe. While I had the opportunity of an empty house, I asked my sister to help me look for it. We searched where everyone else's birth certificates and passports were kept. It wasn't there. I remember thinking to myself, *This psycho probably burnt it to pretend I don't exist.*

During our search, I came across my old school reports. "Let's read these, this will be fun." I laughed to Kiara. They were from Year 1 to Year 6 of primary school, so that would have been the age of 5 to 11 years old. I started off reading them full of enthusiasm, but what I read next stopped me in my tracks. I started flipping through the papers in disbelief. Kiara was confused and asked what was wrong.

"It is a great shame your daughter is being deprived of the education to which she is entitled. Please think carefully about what you are doing to your daughter. She cannot repeat this time. Her future is in your hands," I read to my sister. "This bitch never sent me to school," I expressed.

I felt all of the emotions I had been holding in towards my mother over the last few months, exploding inside me. I felt sick. My average attendance for the school year was 33%. I stayed up all night reading all the reports over and over. Each year repeated my poor attendance. I just couldn't comprehend why she would do this. Although I knew I had a lot of time off school when I was younger, I didn't realise it was this bad. Things were starting to make more sense.

One of the reports mentioned a social worker. That must have been the time my mother scared me into not saying anything, when I was having the meeting at school. I honestly believed I was always ill. My mother had dragged me to the hospital on more than one occasion. I was constantly prodded and poked by doctors. They ran test after test, scan after scan. I even remember them saying to my mother, "We really do not know what is wrong with her." Now that I have discovered these reports, I was hearing a different story.

The morning after my discovery, I woke up thinking it was all a dream, until I saw those green pieces of paper next to me. We were due to go to my friend's house; where my mother was staying, as my sister was going to watch the dogs while my mother went out. *How was I going to face this woman?* I've lasted this long, it will be fine. I could feel the end of my sentence coming. I decided to have a shower at my friend's house, as it was nicer than the one at my mother's.

When we arrived, I sat and had a conversation with my mother for a while, through gritted teeth, of course. Before she left, I asked her for a towel so I could have a shower. She came out with a kids Disney towel, she held it up saying, "Sorry, this is the only towel I could find, she doesn't have any proper towels." I told her it was fine and she hung it up in the bathroom for me.

After I jumped out of the shower, I grabbed the towel and threw it around myself. The stench I was greeted by literally made me heave and I dropped the towel in disgust. It smelt like a wet dog that had dried and then had become wet again. I pinched a corner of the towel and picked it up to examine it. My mother had given me the dog's towel. Even from a distance you could smell how bad it was. I jumped back in the shower and then shouted to Kiara to bring me Kane's towel.

It could have been an easy mistake, so I excused it and went into the bedroom to get dressed. As soon as I walked in, I saw a huge pile of big, fluffy, clean towels and my mother's pyjamas were folded up and sat on top of them all. She knew exactly what she had done! She had strategically told me that was the only towel she could find, knowing full well it was the dog's towel. When she got back, I imagined myself smashing her head against a brick wall again. I needed to shake out of it, but I also wanted to get her back for what she had done.

I saw her lip gloss on the table. It was one of those you applied with a little brush. I picked it up and called my dog over. I gave his teeth the best clean they have ever had with that lip gloss brush and placed it back into the container. When she came back into the room, I asked her to try it on, so I could see what the colour looked like. Which she did, whilst I sat there feeling extremely satisfied with myself as I watched her. It was probably quite a spiteful thing to do and I shouldn't have sunk to her level, but surely it was better than smashing her head against a wall?

I went home that night and instantly looked up the details to contact social services. As they had been mentioned in my reports, I knew they would have a record on me. I also knew my rights to request information anyone holds on you. The next morning I received an email back from them to say they were dealing with my request and I would hear back from them within 21 working days. Those were the longest 3 weeks of my life.

CHAPTER 24
THE TRUTH IS UNRAVELING

One day, I came home and saw an extremely large envelope on the doormat. I picked it up, wondering how the postman managed to squeeze it through the letterbox. I knew what was inside though. I ripped it open and stood there in astonishment, at how thick the file was. The file could just about close. It had near 1000 pages in it, if not more. I started to read through it all and nothing prepared me for what I discovered.

I had always known that I didn't really go to school, but I had no idea the extremes to how bad things were. For five years social services were battling with my mother to send me to school, she was taken to court and fined. A warrant was even put out for her arrest when she missed her court date. She continually ignored social services, all those unanswered knocks at the door as a child all made sense now.

The social workers would turn up unannounced as my mother kept missing all the arranged appointments with them. She was totally uncooperative with them. They fought and fought to get me to school, they contacted the doctors about my health, who confirmed it was nothing out of the ordinary, an odd cold here and there, yet nothing that would justify such poor attendance. They arranged medical tests; as my mother insisted I missed so much school due to my stomach aches, so these must have been the appointments I attended when the doctors said they didn't know what was wrong with me. I even had to have a rectum scan, at the young age of 7 years old. Yet nothing could be found wrong with me.

As I read through all of this in disbelief, tears poured down my face, as I learned I was on the child protection register for neglect. *Neglect!* How can a mother disregard my education so far, to the point I am classed as a neglected child? My whole life, I believed neglected children were those who were starved or left out in the cold, never did it cross my mind that there was such a thing as emotional and educational neglect. I grew angry, how could the system let me down for so long too?

How could I be left on a child protection register for five years?! That is basically my entire early years education, just thrown away. Years I could never get back. Things started to make so much sense to me. This was why I had always struggled in large group discussions in school, and even in my personal life. I had spent the best part of my childhood isolated away. The years I should have spent finding the world through that curiosity we have as children, it had all been kept from me. All the years I struggled through secondary school, believing I was stupid because I found it so hard to focus in an academic setting, a setting that had been foreign to me for so many years.

I felt utterly let down, how had this been allowed to continue for so many years? My life was decided by a monthly panel of "professionals" who had assessed my situation and determined the next steps. They spent years threatening court procedures to take me into care, and just when they were about two weeks away from processing them, my mother started to cooperate and the case was closed. Just like that.

Why had no one noticed what was really going on? My second year teacher wrote a report that said "I have no concerns for Kylie's emotional and physical wellbeing as she appears well cared for." Wasn't we always taught to never judge a book by its cover? So, because I looked well on the outside, that should be a feasible reason as to why I wasn't a neglected child.

Only one teacher fought for me - Mrs Seville, she wrote letter after letter to social services and my mother which read, "50% attendance for a 6 year old is appalling, Kylie is a child in need, under the Children's Act, as her development is being impaired."

They also noted that my mother used the passing of my Aunty Angela as an excuse for me being off so much. She confessed she missed Angela and that I was also very close to her. They worried that my mother was keeping me off to support her emotionally, as she described our relationship as more like sisters, as I was very grown up for my age. Considering I was around the age of 5 or 6 at the time, I don't know why anyone took that seriously. What sane adult uses a child this young as their emotional support?

Despite my attendance continuing to deteriorate, my teachers started to believe I was being taught outside of school, since I coped fairly well with the work I was given on the days I was in, and they highlighted that I had the potential to be quite bright, but I couldn't achieve my full capacity at my current attendance levels. However, they continued to argue that when I was seen I did appear to be fine, so they didn't have any serious concerns.

After a few more years on the child protection register, it was noticed that my personality was changing, and I was struggling more and more in school. An educational psychologist carried out tests on me which indicated that at the age of 8, I was underachieving around two and a half years in my reading, spelling, maths and vocabulary development.

Then the lies started to come to light. Remember that meeting I had when social services came to my school and my mother told me that they were trying to take me away, well, there it was in black and white. My mother had told them that they had upset me so much, I had expressed that I would run away if I was taken from her.

The time my mother confronted my teacher about not giving me the main part in the class assembly and then blamed me for embarrassing her, well, that had been noted down too. My mother had been observed being aggressive towards me, finally some clarity for me too. I wasn't overreacting to how she had made me feel that day. It was right there in clear as day, even if nothing was done about it.

My mother had declared that she felt everyone was blaming her for my poor attendance, and claimed it wasn't her fault I was always ill. She stressed that she couldn't force me to go to school. It was at this point, for the first time, I saw it documented that social services believed my mother had psychiatric problems. Sadly, again, it didn't change anything.

I had even been referred for counselling, as my mother was claiming I couldn't sleep. Now, my recollection of counselling was very different to the picture that I was seeing drawn out in front of me. My mother turned up to collect me early from school one day, saying that I had an appointment, I had no idea what for, yet we arrived at this building and was taken straight into a room with a woman who started asking me loads of questions. Instantly, my back was up, as my mother had always made me cautious of authorities that questioned me.

If you remember me mentioning, she spoke a lot about my father and the neighbour who my mother and Mike argued with quite often. Reading through my records, that counselling session suddenly started to make sense. My mother had taken me to the doctors claiming I wasn't sleeping, as I was terrified of the neighbour, she said that I wouldn't leave the house without her and that I wouldn't play outside, as I was scared he would do something to me. My mother hardly ever let me play outside, so that was a blatant lie.

She claimed he was racially abusing us and that we needed to be moved, the plot thickens, she was using me to try and get us moved. Yet, the notes just made me feel more and more let down by the people who were meant to protect me. The doctor's referral stated that I was very moody and weepy and the therapist noted "Kylie looks like a very worried child, what else is upsetting her? She refuses to see me without her mother present and looks to mother to answer any questions asked."

Now, I am no detective, but with all of these pieces put together, I am seeing a child in desperate need for help here. I don't know what hurt more, the fact that I had proven my mother's abuse my whole life wasn't made up, or the fact that the system knew about it and let me down.

Apparently, the reason I never returned to these sessions was because my mother had told them that I was very upset from my first visit and I had refused to come back. They said they would check in later on in the year, which to be fair they did, however my mother ignored the letters, so they closed my referral.

As I finished reading through everything, I sat there for a moment imagining how much more I could have achieved if I had been given the opportunities everyone else had growing up. However, I also felt extremely proud of myself. Being without my core education and still managing to end up tutoring 16-18 year olds. These kids hadn't coped in mainstream school; some of them had extreme behavioural issues, some had given up on themselves and some were about to go to prison. Yet, my uneducated self, tutored them in Math and English and got them through their exams. This is something I will forever hold as my greatest achievement. And this taught me to never let anything stop me from achieving my goals.

All of this newfound knowledge made it even more difficult to not go and confront my mother, but I knew my prison sentence wasn't quite over. It wasn't time to cut ties with her just yet. Kiara was about to leave for University, so Kane was going to need me more now than ever.

CHAPTER 25
CAN I SMASH HER FACE AGAINST A WALL YET?

With it being a few months since my Grandmother's death, my mother and aunts were just about finalising all of my Grandmother's financial affairs; she didn't have a will, but she had made it clear that any money she did have, she wished to be split between her grandchildren.

The sisters all decided that they would split the money between themselves and then distribute it to their own children. My Grandmother didn't have much, so once everything had been split my mother ended up with around £7000. She said she would take Kane on holiday with his money, as he had never been on a holiday, and then the rest of us could have the money to do with what we wish. I never asked for anything, nor was I bothered with getting anything, in my eyes it was just money, and I definitely wasn't going to ask my mother for my share for her to use it against me. So, I sat by for a few weeks expecting her to do the right thing.

During this time, I witnessed my mother go on shopping spree after shopping spree, constantly "treating herself." She still wasn't working, so I suspected having this amount of money in her account went to her head a bit. Shortly after, Kiara had an argument with my mother; I can't recall what about, but my mother turned round to her and said, "You and Kylie aren't getting any of your Grandmother's money. I don't think you deserve it."

I told her to keep the money if it made her feel happy and she needed it that badly to go against what my Grandmother wanted. She started mocking us saying "Oh, sorry, you still think you're better than me. I've got more money in my account than you." I laughed at her and told her to enjoy it, as it wouldn't last long and we would earn more money for ourselves anyway. She was acting like she had just inherited a million pounds.

Like I said, I didn't need the money, but I did think it was unfair that my siblings never saw their share. They were still young, and were studying, so they couldn't go out and earn money like I could. Kane never got that holiday and on the day of dropping Kiara to university she only had £200 to live off for the next 4 months. This is the only thing that made me angry - you would rather have money, that wasn't intended for you, sit in your account and leave your daughter to struggle to manage such a tight budget, when she is just starting off in the next chapter of her education.

It was a lot harder to maintain this "prison sentence" once Kiara had gone to university. I didn't realise how much having her there to vent to kept me sane. Kiara was out of the mayhem and didn't have to deal with my mother's toxicity on a daily basis. I was pleased for her. Yet, it made it difficult when it came to Kane, usually Kiara would meet me with him, so there wasn't too much interaction with my mother and me. Now, whenever I asked to see Kane my mother was always making excuses, like he had a birthday party, or he had homework. Sometimes she would agree for me to see him, then as I was getting ready to collect him, she would message to say that he had been rude to her so he wouldn't be able to see me. Obviously, with Kiara being away now there was no one to pull her up on her lies and she could tell me whatever she wanted.

About a month away from Christmas, Kiara messaged me letting me know that my mother and her had just got into a huge argument about me. My mother had told her that she didn't want me to spend Christmas with them, as she couldn't forget everything that I had done and play happy families. *Was she for real?* Everything I had done? This woman was delusional. She had an affair, and she was the one that was struggling to sit there and pretend with me? Did she ever wonder how hard it was for all of us to pretend with her?! I had nothing to be sorry for, or to even be forgiven for, yet, again she was projecting on me. She told Kiara that as I was 26 years old, I needed to move on with my own life and leave them alone. I wasn't aware that being 26 meant that I was no longer allowed to have a relationship with my family, but, then this is my mother saying this, so I wasn't surprised.

Kiara told my mother she wasn't getting involved and that she should speak to me herself. She told her that she wanted to spend Christmas with her family and that I was her family. My mother didn't care what anyone else wanted. She had a vendetta against me, and there was no one that could get in the way of that.

I had told Kiara that if my mother didn't want me there on Christmas day then she needed to tell me herself. I wasn't going to allow my sister to be stuck in the middle of this, what my mother and I felt about each other had nothing to do with her. We decided I would play dumb and pretend Kiara hadn't told me. That said, my mother messages me saying "I can't move on from all that shit ok."

I replied to her asking her to call me, as she couldn't just send me a message like that without an explanation. She kept avoiding the call and telling me she was busy and that I should speak with Kiara. I wasn't going to give my mother the easy way out. I knew what was coming and I needed to get it all out. I had done my prison sentence and it was time for my release. This was the moment I had been waiting for, and I had never felt stronger than I did in that instant. My mother had finally lost all control of my emotions. I was so ready for this.

After going back and forth with her telling me she couldn't forgive me, I finally convinced her to call me. As I had already started writing this book almost a year prior to this call, I knew I needed to record the conversation. This was about to play a big part in my story.

CHAPTER 26
THE END IS NEAR

THE PHONE RINGS

Me: *Hello…*

Mother: *So, yeah that message, that's just how I feel.*

Me: *Right, well I still don't understand what it is you can't forgive?*

Mother: *Do I really need to remind you? Telling your Grandmother about the affair, messaging Sean's wife.*

Now, if you remember Mike had begged me for days to message Sean's wife when he found out my mother had been having an affair with him.

Me: *Let's just get two things straight. I rung my Grandmother to see if she was okay, she then starts having ago at me, because you had told her a load of lies. So, naturally, I am going to tell her the truth, to clear my name. I had NO intention of even telling her, as she didn't need to know. Secondly, I only messaged the wife because Mike kept begging me to. In the end, I got sick of him breaking down to me every day, so I agreed.*

Mother: *Well, Mike said he didn't even know you had spoken to her.*

Me: *How do you think I got her number?*

Mother: *Kiara gave it to you.*

Me: *I swear on my life that Kiara had nothing to do with it.*

Mother: *Well, someone's lying.*

Me: *What reason do I have to lie, ask Mike now.*

My mother goes into the other room and tells Mike that I was saying he gave me the wife's number. He denied it and said he couldn't remember. As if I hadn't lost enough respect for him already, this was the moment where I lost it all. I couldn't believe he was willing to let my 18 year old sister, his own daughter, take the blame for this. He told my mother I was lying, and at that moment I knew I would never speak to that poor excuse of a man ever again.

Me: *So, the two things you couldn't forgive me for have been addressed. What else?*

Mother: *Don't worry, Mike is getting kicked out tonight.*

Me: *I don't really care what happens between you two. That has nothing to do with me.*

Mother: *Oh yeah, that's you. Only care about yourself.*

Me: *Well, I am the only person I can rely on. So, of course I am going to put myself first.*

Mother: *Your attitude stinks, even Kiara has less respect for me when you are here.*

Me: *That's something you need to take up with Kiara, if that's what you think. Again, that has nothing to do with me.*

Mother: *It's true, even Kevin has said so.*

Me: *Kevin never said that.*

Mother: *Oh, is that your plan? Get inside your brother's head like you did with Kiara?*

Me: *I didn't get into anyone's head. Kiara has her own mind and opinions.*

Mother: *Well, this thing you have with Kiara is going to stop.*

Me: *What? A relationship with my sister?*

Mother: *You are not welcome in my house anymore. You only come here to see Kane. It's quite clear you don't like me.*

Me: *Obviously, I only come to see Kane, he is 6 years old. I want to have a relationship with my brother.*

Mother: *Well, you can see him once a month. You've had your visit with him this month, so you can see him just before Christmas.*

This was absolutely fine by me. I only put up with my mother for the sake of seeing Kane, so this setup couldn't be better for me.

Mother: *When your Grandmother died, you used that as your way to worm back in and I never wanted that.*

Me: *I didn't try and worm my way back in. I just wanted to see my brother.*

She went on to say that I was only sticking around for the money, I asked how this could be possible when at the time I told her I didn't want it and to keep it. I could tell that my calmness was starting to irritate my mother, that ticking time bomb that I had witnessed so many times as a child was about to explode.

Mother: *You know, I've done so much for you and this is how you treat me!*

Me: *This is another thing I'm trying to get my head around. You keep going on about all that you have done for me. What is it exactly that you have done for me?*

Mother: *I CLOTHED YOU!! I FED YOU!!!*

My patience was starting to wear thin by this point, and I couldn't hold in my calmness anymore. I had been gathering my evidence for months and it was time to use it and be rid of this woman for good.

Me: *BUT YOU DIDN'T SEND ME TO SCHOOL THOUGH, DID YOU?!?*

Mother: *Why didn't you go to school? Because you were always ill.*

Me: *So, I wasn't on the child protection register for neglect, no?*

Mother: *You were never on a register.*

Me: *Stop lying, I have a whole file of evidence sitting in my room from Social Services. It's all there in black and white.*

Mother: *Whatever, you need help. You have mental health problems making something like that up.*

Me: *WOW. You are the one that needs help. You need to go and get your head checked.*

Mother: *You really do have 100% of the crazy gene. You need help.* ***LAUGHING***

Me: *So, you wasn't taken to court and fined? I wasn't almost taken into care? Lie all you want mother, because at the end of the day, we both know the truth and I have a clear conscience.*

Mother: *Yeah, so do I. You're crazy!*

Me: *You know what? You're the only person in the world that thinks these things about me, and I don't value your opinion. So, I don't care what you think.*

Mother: *Well, I know the real you!*

Me: *You know nothing about me. You seriously need help, this is not going to get any better. You are not well in the head. Get out more, get some friends, it's not healthy to live like this.*

My mother starts screaming at me. She is hysterical. Telling me she has loads of friends. She starts reeling off a list of names of people that do not talk to her anymore. I ask her to tell me someone who is still her friend. She couldn't, so she just starts attacking me again.

Mother: *Who do you think you're talking to? You are never to step foot over my doorstep again, do you hear? And don't think you are ever seeing Kane again. I wish I never had you, I should aborted you when I had the chance.*

Me: *If it meant having you as my mother, then I wish you had too! You carry on using Kane as your weapon. When he's older he will hate you just as much as I do. You will drive him away too. Then who will you control?*

Mother: *I don't control anyone.*

Me: *You are controlling Kane right now.*

Mother: *Well, take me to court! Cause you're not seeing him.*

My mother always knew how to push my buttons and she knew that stopping me from seeing Kane would do that.

Me: *You low life piece of scum. You are going to mess that little boy up so much.*

Mother: *Yeah, cause I'm going to neglect him, I forgot, like I neglected you.*

Me: *You really are a crazy bitch!*

Mother: *How dare you call me a crazy bitch!! You better watch yourself, because things are going to start happening to you.*

PHONE CUTS OFF

I sat there for a minute, digesting what had just happened. That was such an intense conversation, with so much anger. I didn't feel sad, or hurt. I felt relieved, a weight had been lifted. The 21st November 2014, for the first time in my life, I was free.

I knew, this time, this would be it, something just felt different. There would be no going back this time. This would be the end of me and her. And even though this was one of the best decisions I had ever made in my life, it also came with one of the hardest… Kane.

It tore me up inside knowing that walking away from my mother and all of her abuse, meant leaving behind one of the people I loved most. However, I knew I couldn't be the big sister Kane would one day need, if I stayed around my mother. And even though Kiara and Kevin were older, I knew it was going to be tough on them too. I was the oldest, so I had always been the one to take on the brunt of my mother's abuse. I was the scapegoat, putting myself in place to protect them.

CHAPTER 27
ADAPTING TO MY NEW NORM

For as long as I had remembered, I had been in survival mode, fighting through life, a battle every day to try and be loved. I had been searching in the wrong place though. I was never going to get the love I so desperately desired from my mother. She was incapable of love. I had spent the best part of my life with an emptiness in my heart, longing for that mother's love. I often questioned if it was something I had done wrong, *how could I make her love me? If only I could be a better daughter.* I used to actually apologise to her for not being good enough, for being difficult. But, I hadn't, I had been the best daughter I could be, she just never wanted to accept it. Even towards the end, I tried so hard; when it was her birthday I offered to take her to the spa for the day, but I was shut down with "I couldn't think of anything worse than spending the day alone with you."

It was over, but the heartache was still there. I had grieved for my mother, for the idea of what I wanted her to be. I had grieved her for so many years, so to walk away from her now, that was the easy part. However, to walk away from my siblings, that was hard. I really did feel like I had let them down. In hindsight, I know walking away was the best thing I did for them though, as I was able to grow, to heal and to become their strong big sister, who stuck her middle finger up to anything and anyone that tried to break her down.

Adjusting to this new way of life was strange, but there is one woman that made it so much easier to handle, and that was Roe. The mother I had longed for my whole life, I had found in her. She loved me as if I was her own; she was there for me on my good days and my bad days. She cried with me and laughed with me. I told her everything. I had literally manifested her. I used to go to bed as a child and fantasise about being an adult; living in a big house, with a grand staircase, imagining my wedding day, walking down those stairs, surrounded by so many people who loved me, with a mother who adored the ground I walked on, stood right beside me.

Roe truly was the mother I had always dreamt of. My mother had always been jealous of my relationship with Roe, she used to try and say that it was weird and tell people I was obsessed with her and that I was in love with her. Yet, I see now why Roe was such a threat to her. She showed me that I was a good daughter. I was capable of being loved. There were never any judgements, I was able to make mistakes and she was always there to wipe away my tears, to push me through me fears and celebrate all of my wins. If anyone asks me who my mother is now, I will always tell them it's Roe.

The first Christmas after I went no contact with my mother was weird, even though I had spent most Christmas' with Natalie, I would usually go to hers in the evening for dinner and spend the morning with my siblings. So, being away from them was extremely difficult. I had so many people that would invite me to spend Christmas with them, but it just felt like I was the spare piece to a puzzle and I was an observer of their Christmas. It wasn't my Christmas.

I used to love Christmas so much, it was my favourite time of the year. I would be that annoying festive person, with tinsel earrings and a Santa hat. However, since that first Christmas away from my siblings, it was never the same, the magic had gone and I had turned into your typical bah humbug. Every year leading up to the festivities, I dread it. Everyone heading home for the day, but all I wanted, I wouldn't get, so it wasn't a time to celebrate for me.

My second Christmas after going no contact, was approaching fast and the anxiety it filled me with was immense. I really couldn't handle another Christmas of pretending I was okay being away from my siblings, I just wanted to be away to forget it all. So, I booked myself a flight to Dubai and flew out by myself a few days before Christmas. My friends couldn't believe I was going alone. They were convinced I was meeting someone out there.

My Aunty Sarah facetimed me on Christmas Eve crying, saying that I shouldn't be alone for Christmas and that I should be there with them. It wasn't anything personal to anyone else, I just didn't want to be around anyone. I did a lot of reflecting during that solo trip. It had been just over a year since I had stopped speaking to my mother, and I felt so grateful, things were going well for me. I was happy, I was loved and I was flourishing. My whole mindset had shifted. I had been consumed by negativity my entire life, now that I was free from it, I was finally starting to see things from a new perspective.

I had always worried that I would turn out like my mother, bitter and angry at the world, but being away from her had really taught me how to see the positive in a situation. Everything has a silver lining. She had taught me to hold on to grudges, but I learnt how to forgive.

Dubai was amazing. Christmas day, I slept on the beach after spending the day at the Atlantis water park. This was what freedom felt like, no walking on eggshells around my mother whilst she cooked the dinner, no anxiety over not showing enough excitement for my presents to be told I was ungrateful, no arguments over setting the dinner table, only for my mother to refuse to eat with us anyway and storm out of the kitchen whilst the rest of us ate, causing an atmosphere you wouldn't associate with Christmas dinner.

Things felt a little lighter when I got back. Don't get me wrong the pain was still there, I don't think the pain will ever go away; I was just outgrowing the pain. The more I grew as a person the smaller it got. I was working at KidZania at this time. It was a miniature city for kids, a replica of the real world where kids could role play jobs and earn money for them. We were having a special event and there was a select number of tickets available for free. I told Kiara to let my mother know so that Kane could come and enjoy the day. My mother took the offer up and brought Kane. I was walking around the city with one of my work colleagues, secretly hoping I would see Kane. Just as I walked upstairs, I saw my mother and Mike. She looked me dead in the face and carried on walking.

I turned to my colleague and said, "You see that woman that just walked passed us? That's my mother."

She replied "But she just walked past you like you're a stranger." I nodded.

I had already told her about the situation with my mother, but I found that most people just didn't understand. I didn't expect them to. It is hard for people to get their head around the one person that is meant to love you more than anything, hating you. People can only understand what they can relate to, so I found myself being very limited with the information I shared beyond that point. Until one evening where I was sat up having a deep late night conversation with Natalie, where I started to delve a little deeper into the relationship with my mother. Natalie had always known things weren't good with us, and she had been the one that was there while I was going through my no contact. She had seen all the tears, all the arguments and she had seen the broken version my mother had created of me. Something that evening just made me open up, like I had never opened up before. Explaining my childhood and the things I had been through, things that I had thought were normal behaviours, Natalie sat there in disbelief with her mouth wide open.

"Your mum sounds like a narcissist," she replied and she quickly grabbed her phone scrolling through Google, before she forwarded me an article on Narcissistic mothers.

As I read through it I thought, *Wow, it's like someone has tapped into my brain and is writing my life story out.* For the first time in my life, I found a place I belonged, a place I felt heard and understood. It was this moment that I realised. *It isn't just me! It wasn't my fault. I am not alone!*

Natalie headed to bed and I spent the rest of the evening falling down a rabbit hole, reading other people's experiences and I found great comfort in their stories, it really is true when they say "one person's story is another person's survival guide." I had taken a 3 year break from writing this book at that point, but after the comfort I felt going through these articles, I felt inspired to get back to writing and to get my story out there, if I could provide the same comfort I had felt to at least one person out there, then I would be happy.

CHAPTER 28
I AM NOT ALONE

I started up a Facebook page and put my first blog post out there, talking about what a narcissistic mother is and the effects mine had on me. I was overwhelmed by the response I received. People from all over the world were messaging me, telling me what an inspiration I was, how I had given them the strength to push through, but most importantly, so many people messaged me thanking me for helping them realise that they were not alone. I had found my life purpose, and I needed to turn my pain into something positive and provide a safe community for all of the people that could relate to my story.

I continued to do my research on Narcissistic mothers so I could raise awareness of the topic in a way that was also going to be gentle and help others heal. It was like I had found the user guide to my mother and everything was making sense. I discovered that Narcissists will criticise you any opportunity they get, even in the most subtle way. I remember my mother never told me that I was doing well, my exams for example, she never encouraged me, or congratulated my results, instead she would tell me how good someone else had done and ask why I can't be more like them. I could relate this scenario to so many different situations in my life.

There are NO boundaries when living with a Narcissistic mother, she will invade your privacy in ways you could never imagine. I thought back to when my mother hacked into my Facebook and when she used to sit in my room and listen to my telephone conversations.

Narcissistic mothers have their "favourites." My mother always preferred the boys. I realised from a very young age I became the scapegoat of the family; the one that always got the blame and she was always bending the truth to make me look like the bad guy to everyone else, like when she turned her affair on me, remember how she tried to turn everyone against me to cover up her lies.

Narcissists hate to see you happy. Anytime my mother saw me on a high or knew I was about to go somewhere that I was excited about, she would pick a fight with me. She knew it would ruin my mood and consume my mind for the rest of the day and I wouldn't be able to enjoy what I was originally excited about.

Narcissists will never admit the way they treat you. The amount of times I confronted my mother about her actions and the way they had made me feel, for her to turn around and tell me she didn't know what I was talking about. I have actually lost count of the amount of times I had been told by her that I was "too sensitive" or "always taking everything to heart."

Another common trait of a narcissist is to make you believe you are crazy. She always made me doubt myself and I would be sat there asking myself, *Did that really happen? Did I blow that out of proportion?* Researching all of this made me realise, *No, I'm NOT crazy. Her behaviour is not okay*!

Narcissists are very jealous. If you get something nice or if someone does something nice for you; they will find a way to spoil it. Remember when I booked my trip to The Bahamas with Natalie, my mother picked a fight to ruin my excitement. At the time, I couldn't understand why she was starting on me, but I got it now.

Narcissists love to lie too! The majority of things that came out of my mother's mouth were lies. Her lies were more obvious to me, but to other people she would pre-empt her lies, so that she can't be caught out. Like the time she told my aunt that she had been rushed into hospital to have her appendix out, just because she didn't want to look after my younger cousin.

They feed off your pain. Anytime anything happened to upset me, she would twist the knife and make the pain ten times worse. Narcissists are "Emotional Vampires". They love to see you cry. I remember when I had an argument with my first boyfriend, my mother got involved and filled my head full of insecurities and then called him up and cussed him, but not in a caring mother way, in an embarrassing way that made me never want to speak to him again.

They are extremely selfish. Always having to have things their way. I had too much experience with this one, if things didn't go the way my mother wanted them to, then that "Narcissistic Rage" would come out. Her needs were always a priority, yet she would remind me at any given chance that I was the selfish one.

And don't even get me started on constructive criticism. The older I got and the more I begun to value my life I knew to avoid any kind of criticism, otherwise she would get extremely defensive and start telling me that I never thought she was good enough, because she is uneducated and I thought I was better than her. These were words that had never come out of my mouth, but were always her go to comeback.

Another trait she ticked the box for was her childish behaviours, she was worse than a 6 year old; she would hold a grudge for the longest time and would always be plotting how to get her own back. I remember she fell out with her sister once over something probably extremely silly, but my mother decided that this was enough for her to get a burner phone, to send abusive messages to her sister and signed her up to a load of funeral services, so that she would receive funeral brochures through the post. Like how twisted did you have to be to even muster up something like that?

Narcissistic mothers will also "parentify" you at the first opportunity they get. By now, you all know how I was a mother of two at the age of 9, when I was expected to do everything for my younger siblings.

And they will never accept when they are in the wrong. Oh, how I could relate to this! My mother never done anything wrong, there would never be an apology, because she was mightier than God, and nothing would ever be her fault; even her affair was my fault. Understanding the definition of a scapegoat at this point had never felt so good. It was like I could suddenly put all the puzzle pieces together and see the bigger picture. I still had a lot to learn about the topic, but I had a cheat sheet now, to get out of this toxic space and really begin to break the generational curse and heal from years of trauma.

I didn't feel guilty for walking away anymore, I had often wondered if cutting her off was a result of my selfishness, as I was leaving my siblings to deal with her demonic ways, but discovering all this new knowledge on narcissism, I realised there was only so much emotional abuse and heartache I could put up with. She was venomous.

CHAPTER 29
I FINALLY FOUND MY VOICE

For my own sanity, there was no way I could continue to let her inflict so much pain on me. So, I vowed to myself that from that day forward I would shout my story from the rooftops to raise awareness to all the people out there, who, like me, thought they are the only ones in this situation. To all the people out there who had said to me "but you only get one mother in life." To all the people out there who had said "this is just her way, she still loves you."

I learnt that I shouldn't feel ashamed or embarrassed of my story. Instead, I should be proud for everything I had achieved in life, despite having an evil, manipulative, twisted woman who stood behind me for most of my life, trying to break me down.

As much as I wasn't ashamed of my story anymore, I still felt the need to protect my identity and wouldn't reveal who I was to my followers, on my private social pages however I was very open about this being my story, it got me thinking back to when my mother hacked my Facebook and I wondered if she had discovered my blog. Although my security settings were super high on my social pages, the link to my blog was in all my bios, so she could have easily found it.

I knew my mother still tried to find ways to get information about me. She and Kiara got into arguments about me because Kiara was refusing to feed my mother's need to know what was happening in my life.

I don't know why the thought of her finding my blog made me feel like I had done something wrong. I knew how mad she would be that I was sharing the truth. I wondered if I should remove it, but why should I hide? If she wants to obsess over me, then so be it. After a few days of guilt, I reminded myself that it was her that should feel ashamed not me and that if she did stalk my profile and decide to read the blog, then I should give her something to read. So, I dedicated the following post for her to read:

"Dear Mother,

Or should I say womb donor, as this is all I see you as now.

*I tried for so many years to please you, to love you and to get you to love me back. All I ever wanted was the love of a mother. However **YOU** didn't want any of this. I blamed myself for the longest time; maybe if I had been a better daughter, things would have been different? Things never would have been different though, as I have discovered you are unlovable! You say I am the one who has hated you for years, and that you have always known, yet what I think really happened here is that you taught me how to hate. I wouldn't know what hate felt like without you in my life!*

You will never see the error of your ways, you think you are perfect and that everyone else is the problem. Yet, you are the problem. You are the one that people can't stand to be around. No matter how many times you tried to tell me that I was ungrateful and selfish, I still had people around me to tell me otherwise. And quite frankly, I couldn't care less what you think about me now, as your opinion is not one that I value. So, think what you want. At the end of the day we both know the truth.

You are a twisted, malicious, evil, pathetic excuse of a mother. You don't even deserve the right to be called this. I spent 8 years hating you with every ounce of my body, until 2 years ago when I realised that you are not worth poisoning my body for. You are nothing to me. I loved you and you broke that; way before I was even old enough to realise it. I was lucky enough to find the motherly love I had always desired in other people, you will never know what that feels like.

I did care once. I'm not a monster like you, however you tore me up inside and almost destroyed me, but you failed because I came bouncing back, stronger than ever. You thought I would be weak without you, you thought I wouldn't survive. Oh how wrong you were.

I used to look at other people and wish I had a mother like theirs. Someone to hug me, tell me they loved me, be there to hold me when I felt like my world was crashing down. I grieved for all of what I didn't have, but my grief is over now. You are dead to me. I don't hate you anymore. I feel nothing.

Stood next to you in the supermarket (I know you think I didn't see you) I felt nothing. You were just another stranger. I will continue to walk past you in the street as if you don't exist, your future grandchildren will also walk past you in the street and won't even know who you are. I will be sure to protect them from you!

All the mind games you tried to play for all these years, by dangling my baby brother in my face, have only made me stronger. You always used him as a weapon, but you have run out of ammo now. As I know when he is older he will come and find me. You cannot break me anymore. No matter what you try to do. I have become immune to you.

Go and cry and badmouth me to anyone you have left to listen, I do not care. You brought this on yourself, through all the abuse I put up with for all these years. I know you won't call it abuse, because ~~you didn't beat me~~. Let me rephrase that, you barely beat me.

You think I am a horrible person for treating you this way? After all that you have done for me? We have already established you are no mother of mine. I won't wish you well, as I am not a liar. I hope you rot in eternal hell.

And just so you know, I'm doing SO good without you…
Sincerely not yours.
Kylie"

I contemplated whether to post the blog for days, but when I finally pressed that post button, it felt like a huge middle finger up to my mother. I felt like I had won, I had control now! She no longer had the power to affect me. I had survived. Or so I thought.

CHAPTER 30
MY ONE WEAKNESS, KANE

On Kane's 9th birthday, I got a call from my sister. I answered it and she said Kane wanted to talk to me. My heart sank. He came on the phone and I instantly got a lump in my throat. I hadn't heard his voice in almost two years.

"Can I see you today?" he asked. I was so confused, I knew he wouldn't ask that without it being agreed with my mother; he knew better than to ask to see me.

"Of course," I said excited.

He continued to say, "Great, we're going to get pancakes in about an hour, so what time should we meet you?"

I started to feel uneasy about this, so I asked, "Who's coming?" As soon as I heard him say "mummy" I told him I would arrange it with Kiara.

When my sister came back on the phone I was livid. "You can't just put me in a situation like that"

She cut me off and quickly said, "Ok, cool. I'll speak to you in a bit," then hung up.

I sat there in disbelief. This woman still knew just how to get me. Kiara messaged me to say sorry, that my mother had told her to ring me right away without warning me beforehand, she had then stood there the whole phone conversation.

I told my sister there was no way I would sit in the same room as this woman, but was happy to meet my brother and her after, so I wouldn't have to see my mother. We both knew this wasn't going to go down well but it was worth a shot. We were right though. My mother went into a rage, saying that if I couldn't sit down with her then I couldn't see my brother. She then turned to Kane and said, "See? It's not me stopping her from seeing you. She doesn't want to, not even on your birthday."

Thankfully, Kiara told her that what she had just done was twisted, and she shouldn't say things like that to Kane, as we all knew that I would never have agreed to meet them if she was there.

I was so annoyed that she tried to get to me again; ok, she had got to me. Not her personally, but hearing Kane's voice asking to see me and knowing that he had his hopes shattered on his birthday, this is what broke me. Maybe I should have given in for his sake, and just put myself through the pain of seeing her, but this is what she wanted, she had manipulated the situation to paint me in a bad light.

It had been over two years since this woman had made me cry. I needed to let her know exactly how I felt. I didn't want to break my no contact, but decided sending her a message and then blocking her straight away would just confirm it for me.

So that is exactly what I did, and I sent the following:

"The sooner you get it into your head that I NEVER want to see you again, the better. I told you years ago to stop using Kane as a weapon and you are still trying it. If the only way I can see him is to have to put myself through the torture of seeing your twisted, fucked up, poisonous self; then I will wait until he's older and can make his own choices. YOU ARE DEAD TO ME. Don't mention my name, don't think about me and don't ever speak to me again. Act like I don't exist cause I sure as hell do the same with you."

I don't regret sending it and I don't regret the decision I made to not see Kane, as hard as it was. I'm not happy that this is how things have to be, however if I am going to be the strong sister he is going to one day need, then I need to stay away. I just hoped he doesn't hate me for it, but I have faith that when he's older and understands better he will see why I stayed away. It was to protect him just as much as it was to protect me. I couldn't allow her to have the power to keep ripping me out of his life. It was kinder this way. The last thing I wanted was for him to be in the middle.

After two years of managing my emotions, this episode had triggered me again. It had brought up the pain all over again. One evening shortly after, as I was sat scrolling through Instagram, I saw that my cousin Chad had started an Instagram live, I clicked on it and there he was, with Kane, my heart sunk. He was a different child. I almost didn't recognise this grown up boy. He's not that baby I remember. Chad announced that I had joined the live and Kane's face dropped. I realise it was probably out of fear of my mother finding out that he had "contact" with me, but at that moment in time, I had convinced myself it was because he hated me for leaving him. His eyes used to light up when he saw me, but now he looked so uncomfortable.

I ran out of my room and went to find Natalie in the kitchen. I burst into tears and was in hysterics about how Kane hated me, that I had ruined everything and how different my life would have been if I had just stuck it out and kept my mother around. Sure, I would have been miserable, but at least I would have Kane. She calmed me down and assured me that wasn't the case. She made me realise that the initial shock of seeing him had triggered me to have this meltdown. She reminded me of the progress I had made since cutting my mother off. And I agreed, yet, what hurt most was the fact that my brother was ten minutes down the road from me, at my Aunty's house and she hadn't said anything to me. She could have told me to come over so I could see him. I couldn't get my head around why none of my family members were adult enough to stand up for me. To stand up to my mother and tell her she was being ridiculous. I only had myself to rely on. No one ever fought my corner. They never had and they never will. When I tell you that is one of the loneliest, soul-destroying feelings ever, I'm not joking. Ever since I left home at 19, I had never felt like I belonged in a family. I was always there to fix everyone else's problems, but I was just thrown to the rubbish heap and forgotten about. I used to beg for my Aunties to check in on me from time to time. I would say, "If I don't come home at night, no one knows. I don't have a mum or a dad that checks I'm okay." Yet, my requests always fell on deaf ears, I really was alone.

CHAPTER 31
CRAVING A MOTHER'S LOVE

As this empty feeling grew stronger, I began to feel a strong sense of missing something. I never missed my mother and I still don't miss her personally, but I missed something. Roe was moving away to Spain, so perhaps this triggered this sentiment, but it was a feeling I was struggling to shake. And everywhere I was looking there were people expressing their love for their mothers. I don't feel bitter towards them. I am glad they have mothers they can love unconditionally. It was just starting to feel suffocating. Daily, I was seeing posts on social media about how much we should love our mothers, as we only get one.

These posts infuriate me. Why should I love my mother just because she gave me life? Does giving someone life allow them to put you through years of emotional abuse? Just because she wasn't beating me every day doesn't mean what she was doing wasn't damaging.

Imagine having to go through years of being told you aren't good enough! Years of being purposely isolated! Not being allowed an opinion because nothing you said was ever correct. Years of coming home and being completely ignored; beating yourself up inside wondering what you could have done to upset her. Years of any confidence you had being picked at, breaking you down bit by bit. I should love that?

Yet, still I feel that empty feeling, and I hate that I was allowing myself to have any emotion related to my mother, even though I know it's natural. I just wish that for one day, I could be normal and have a mother that loves me. Just for one day to have a mother's shoulder to cry on and tell me everything is going to be okay. Just for one day to have someone to take care of me for once. I wasn't missing MY mother. I was missing the idea of a mother and I wished just for one day, I had one. As much as I was lucky to have Roe as a substitute throughout my adult life, and she was great at it, she was everything I had ever wished for in a mother, my inner child was still screaming out for the love I had been deprived of growing up.

A few weeks passed and my yearning for that mother figure was starting to fade again, until I became quite unwell. I had a really bad cough and the pain in my side was getting quite bad. I woke up one morning and I knew I needed to stop being so stubborn. So, I called 111 just to see what they suggested. As I spoke to the advisor through my symptoms, she said she was sending an ambulance right away. At that moment the need for a mother came back.

With a combination of pain and fear, I just burst into tears. Luckily, Natalie was with me and her comforting made me feel better. I braved up and told myself I could do this. I messaged my Aunty Sarah who had a day off work and I asked her if she would meet me at the hospital, because I didn't want to be alone.

When the paramedic arrived he did a few tests and asked a few more questions. When he asked me for my next of kin, I hesitated. I've never really thought about this before. Who would I put down? I quickly just gave my cousin Lola's details as she drives and would always be able to get to me quickly.

This question played on my mind the whole way to the hospital. I've been fine living my life without my mother. But all of this time, she has probably been down as my next of kin. Could you imagine her getting the call to make decisions about my life, if God forbid anything was to happen!?

I arrived at the hospital before Sarah. I looked around and saw a young girl waiting with her mother, and an older woman waiting with her son. That ache of needing someone with me started to come back. I was so scared. Not knowing what was wrong with me, or if I was about to be taken into surgery. I was clueless.

After a few tests, I was sent home with antibiotics, turns out I had a mild case of pneumonia, although I was relieved I still wished I had someone to take care of me. Being ill had always been such a struggle for me, as I had never been able to have that mother figure to fuss over me, except for when I was living with Roe. However with her living in Spain now, I went home alone and cried myself to sleep at how difficult the next few days of recovery were about to be for me.

CHAPTER 32
CHANGE OF MINDSET

As I sat in my pity party feeling sorry for myself, I started to reflect a lot on life, I started to look at what this was all trying to teach me, being brought up in such a negative environment, living with my mother, it was always quite hard to see the positive in any situation. However, the longer I went without interaction with her, the easier it became for me to remain a positive person. Don't get me wrong; we all have our bad days, where we feel like the world is going to end. How you deal with those bad days is what's most important though, and is something I feel has truly guided me in life.

Before I became ill, I felt like I was falling back into a mindset I used to adapt when my mother was in my life. I needed to re-align my positivity; so, I took a step back and took this opportunity to just allow some "me time," to help me find solidarity again. During my cocooning, as I like to call it, I started to really evaluate everything around me. From my working situation, to my life goals, I even evaluated the people in my life. I often find my environment massively affects my way of thinking, so, this was definitely an assessment I needed to do on my life.

I started with my job. My current situation had become an extremely toxic environment. It was consuming all my energy. I was literally drained as soon as I woke up in the mornings. I used my time off sick to search for a new job. I had also become a strong believer of the Law of Attraction too, so I knew how important a positive mindset was at this time. I downloaded the audiobook *The Secret,* which I highly recommend if you are unsure how to adapt your way of thinking. I listened to this on repeat everyday whilst I was at home ill and even at my desk when I returned to work. I blocked out all the negativity. If I had to be included in it, I would try and turn it around and get myself to believe it would get better. I told myself every day that it didn't matter how bad it was, because I wasn't going to be there for long.

It wasn't working though. I was still blocking the positivity from coming through. So, this is when I started looking at the people around me. I pretty much went AWOL from everyone. I needed to focus on me and only me. I am a sucker for making someone else's problems my problems. Probably from years of prioritising my mother's needs over my own, I had become a people pleaser. I needed to set some boundaries, now it was time to say, "Sorry you are going through that, I hope YOU figure it out." It may sound selfish and I most definitely annoyed a lot of people in this time. However, the people that brought the positive energy I required to my life, understood and gave me my space. Anyone that didn't, I began to ask myself what value they were actually bringing to my life and if it was wise to keep them around.

Saying this makes me sound like a terrible person, and I sometimes worried I was turning out just like my mother, a narcissist that only cares about herself, but honestly, I had spent my whole life putting other people's feelings first. It was time to stop. Now that I had put all negativity aside, I was finally able to focus solely on my first mission, to find a new job. I started listening to positive affirmations on YouTube while I slept. Within a week, I had found the perfect role, interviewed for it AND got offered the job! Some might say it's coincidence, but I honestly believe it was the Law of Attraction. I mean I even wrote my resignation letter before I had found out I had the job. I believed it would happen and it did.

Being no contact with my mother for three years at this point, I knew the pros of cutting certain people off. It also meant I could cut anyone out. If I can do it with the person that gave me life, what made people think I wouldn't do it with them? If anyone came to me on a downer, it was bye bye. Now, I'm not heartless, people do have bad days! We all do. However, the people that liked to hold on to those bad days, feeding off the drama and refusing to let go of it, these were the people that had to go. I had no time for anyone that wanted to dwell in the past and not learn and grow from it. I was taking my past and trying to turn my traumas into lessons and guides to grow as a person. I want to take every hurdle that tries to break me and learn from them. I couldn't relate to anyone that didn't want that for themselves, so I had a real life detox. I felt like a new woman!

I find it so important to take some time out to just focus on yourself, especially when things get too much, I think it's easier for me to say because I'm a massive introvert, so I love my alone time. Yet, in a world as busy and crazy as the one we live in, you need to look after you! Turn your phone off, meditate, recharge your batteries. Whatever works for you.

I realised how important it is to grow from the downfalls in life. If you don't you will get consumed in a ball of negativity and it will start to affect every aspect of your life. Hey, for some, you may not mind it or believe it. Me, I just want to get the best I can out of life. I wasted more than half of my lifetime letting my suffering consume me. So, it was important to surround myself with people who had the same views on self-development and healing, but at the same time appreciating that healing isn't straight forward, you don't heal overnight. It is a tough journey, but a journey worth taking.

CHAPTER 33
HEALING WOUNDS

During my deep dive into my pain, I started to think about my one true pain, the pain that I still struggled to deal with - Kane. It was approaching his 10th birthday and it was another year I wouldn't be celebrating with him. Not seeing him has definitely been the hardest part of going no contact with my mother.

Ten years of life. It seemed like only yesterday when he was born. I wondered what he was like now. Was he still that funny, cheeky trickster he used to be? What does he like? Who are his friends? What traits does he have?

Although Kiara would tell me stuff about him from time to time. I tried not to ask too much because it just upset me. It's like I don't even know who he is anymore. I hoped he didn't feel the same way about me and forget about me! I couldn't believe my baby was ten. So grown up, but, as sad as it made me, it just meant he was one year closer to being able to make his own decisions.

This was the only thing that kept me fighting strong. I just hope when the time comes he hasn't been moulded into my mother.

Despite me missing Kane; a feeling that will never be lessened, things were going well. I was thriving in my career, I was about to turn thirty, a whole new decade, one untarnished by my mother, a clean canvas. I had learnt a lot and been through a lot in my twenties, so I was excited for this new chapter. And it started well, I was in a good place mentally, I had good people around me. I had started my own business and was working towards growing that. Life was good. I was happy. Yet, every time I got too happy, it was like the Universe had another test for me, to see if I really was content, and I would get pushed right back into the firing zone. Everything I had fought for to get me to where I was, had been questioned.

I even found myself having a moment of madness and actually considered just letting my mother back into my life in order for me to make situations easier. But, then like a Rafiki in The Lion King moment, it hit me. And I came to my senses again.

Kiara had been at university for the past four years and was soon to be graduating. Her graduation had been a moment I had been worrying about since going no contact with my mother, as I knew it would be the day I had to come face to face with her.

As the time drew closer, it was making me feel so anxious, so I asked my sister if our Aunty Sarah could come with me. All was fine and Sarah had agreed she would come to be my support. She didn't speak to my mother at this point, so she understood completely how her presence can make someone feel.

Everything changed though. A few weeks before the graduation Kiara called me and explained that she didn't think it would be a good idea for Sarah to come, as it would annoy our mother. Now, I understood why she was saying this, my mother would have taken her anger out on her, and she didn't want that on her graduation. So, to keep the peace and to keep our mother from exploding into a rage, she asked I come alone.

Not going with Sarah I could understand, but why couldn't I bring someone else? Kiara was adamant that she wanted no one else there. I kind of understood her reasoning behind this and I don't hold any feelings towards her - she's my sister. I love her and respect her decisions. However I couldn't help but feel hurt that she would allow me to feel unhappy in order to keep her mother happy.

The thought alone of having to face this woman by myself sent me into a meltdown. I felt emotions I hadn't felt in well over three years. I couldn't do it to myself again. I've come so far in my journey since cutting her off. If this was the way she made me feel just thinking about having to see her, then there was no way I was going to allow her to be near me. That's too much negative energy for my liking. So, I told Kiara I would not be attending. As much as it burned me inside to miss my sister's big day, I had to put my mental health first, and there was no way I was about to undo my hard work for anything.

And that is exactly what I did from that point forward. My mental health was the most important thing to me. If I wasn't feeling how something was making me feel, I let it go, whether it was people, jobs, places. I stopped entertaining things that were draining me.

CHAPTER 34
EMBRACING AUTHENTICITY

I think this was when my healing journey really started, although I believed it had started the day I cut my mother off. It really didn't start until I was around 34 years old. It wasn't until I started to really get to the raw pain I had, started to recognise what my triggers were and why they triggered me. My nervous system had been damaged and it was going to take time to rewire it. Things would always trigger me, but it was time to learn how to deal with those triggers.

I started to realise I had PTSD from my childhood and even from my early adulthood. The first time I realised this was when I was staying over at my friend Arianna's house. I had met Arianna just after lockdown and she had very quickly become a sister figure in my life. I had never met someone who had such a genuine interest for everyone's wellbeing. She made me feel safe, her aura oozed a warm, loving energy. Just being in her presence was healing.

One morning I was asleep and Arianna had woken up before me and started putting the dishes away in the cupboards. The sound of crashing plates and slamming cupboards instantly startled me and I jumped out of my sleep. I was on high alert, and instantly felt a rush of fear filling my entire body. I didn't understand at first, then I realised, whenever my mother was about to start on me, she would slam cupboards and put the dishes away aggressively; only people that can relate will understand the sound of an aggressive plate being put in a cupboard.

I rushed into the kitchen and asked Arianna if she was okay, I thought I had done something wrong, so I did what I had done best my entire life - I entered survival mode, as a child I had quickly learnt that to ease my mother's rage, I had to make her happy. I turned to Arianna and told her to leave the plates and I would put them away. I felt guilty for not doing them the night before, was she mad because they hadn't been put away yet? She turned and looked at me confused, "Why are you awake? It's 5am?" I explained to her how the noise had triggered me and she apologised, saying she was just trying to quickly put everything away before she went to work, so that I wouldn't do it when I was up.

If you knew the sense of relief I felt in that moment, you would think I had just been given the all clear on a life threatening disease, my brain had been conditioned to assess for potential threats, and as a result I had become hypervigilant to reading the energy of people around me. I could tell Arianna was genuinely unaware of the stress she had caused, but she did take on board what I had tried to explain and the next time I heard her putting the dishes away early in the morning, I could tell she was doing it as quietly as she possibly could. And that was another reason why I knew, I was safe around her.

Another one of my triggers was the silent treatment, this was quite possibly one of my worst "punishments" as a child and it terrified me! Due to being hyper sensitive, having the ability to read a room and sense a shift in the environment, I usually knew when someone was upset or annoyed; and the silence that usually came after that would send me into a spiral, my mind would be doing summersaults, putting two and two together and coming back with ten. I would create a million different scenarios in my head as to why this person could be mad at me, things I could have said differently, so that I didn't trigger them.

This is when the people pleasing would be at its finest. I always knew my mother wouldn't be as mad at me, if I made her happy. I didn't realise how much of this I had brought into my adult life. Yes, people get silent when they are upset, but it didn't mean it had anything to do with me. However, I would still convince myself it was. This would then lead onto insomnia, and I would keep myself up at night playing the conversation over and over in my head trying to figure out where I had gone wrong.

The silent treatment is still one thing to this day that can take me back to that 8 year old girl, standing helplessly, doing everything in my power to try and fix the mess I had made with my mother; trying to put right what I had done wrong, walking on eggshells, analysing my mother's mood to see when the right time would be to carry out my "fix it" plan. I could tell what mood my mother was in by the sound of her sighs, the way she ate her food and even the sound of her footsteps.

I can't tell you how many times I ran to the top of my bunk beds and pretended to be asleep because my mother's footsteps sounded angry. I didn't realise until recently that footsteps shouldn't have moods.

I spent a lot of my childhood in fantasy land, lying in bed imagining my life as an adult, the love that surrounded me, the support, the children I had that I loved unconditionally and gave everything I had always wished for. Never for a second did I realise, this was my brain blocking out the pain I was enduring in my everyday life. This was my brain dissociating from reality.

Nothing I ever did was good enough for my mother. She never told me she was proud, I always felt like I should have done more, I was constantly letting her down. I didn't realise this had caused me to self-sabotage in my adult life, that it made me fear success. I knew how to be a failure, so that almost became my coping mechanism. I know what to expect if I fail, but I didn't know how to deal with success. Even writing this book, I almost self-sabotaged it. I questioned if I deserved success, would anyone care? Perhaps I was overreacting and things weren't as bad as I had thought? I doubted my own pain, because I told myself other people had it worse than me. Trauma is trauma, no one should have to feel like they can't grieve for the life they never had, we should be allowed to feel our pain and not feel judged or victim blamed. I've lost count the amount of times I've been told that my mother abused me because she had her own traumas, and maybe if I understood what hers were then I would accept mine more. Hurt people don't hurt people, evil people hurt people. This is a poor excuse for her behaviour and just enables abusers more when people tell them this. I would NEVER put a child through what I went through, it makes me sick to my stomach the thought of any child having to feel the way I felt growing up.

People think because you can't see the wounds of an emotional abuse victim, then they aren't as damaging, yet, what they don't realise is these wounds stay with us for life. They are embedded in us, our entire being has been conditioned into believing we are worthless. We spend our lives craving kindness, as we were deprived of it for so long, in turn, creating a "something for something" mentality, nothing nice ever came without me needing to repay it or it would be thrown back in my face. So, now I find it hard to accept nice gestures, it feels weird for me to not repay the kindness. And this caused me to become terrified of disappointing people. I had been conditioned to never let my mother down, so, I grew up feeling bad if I didn't break my back for the people around me after they had been good to me.

As a society, we need to be more aware of emotional abuse and the effects it has. As a survivor, trying to speak my truth for the best part of sixteen years, when you aren't heard or are told "but they did their best", it cuts deep and makes you feel completely isolated, foolish, ashamed and alone; it is not okay. As a society, we need to do better. Don't underestimate the power of just listening.

Aside from Arianna, my good friends Laura and Xena also played a big part in my healing journey. Like I said my journey didn't really start until I was 34 years old, and that was because of these girls. Being able to speak my truth, with no judgements, no interruptions, no buts, just genuine care and love, allowed me to heal more than I realised I needed to. Just saying things out loud permitted me to process a lot and identify why I was the way I was and what my triggers were.

I didn't realise how much I had held in, until I was able to speak about it in a safe space, with no one telling me I needed to let it go. It also helped them to understand my triggers and see them before I did, they would know what could send me into a spiral and they would catch me before I fell and if I did fall they would hold me until I was ready to get back up again. I have cried my eyes out around these girls, set up camp on their sofas for weeks at a time; when I've been too low to even take care of myself, and even got myself silly drunk and fallen asleep on Arianna's shower floor.

For the first time in my life, I allowed myself to be truly vulnerable, let my guard down and feel my deepest, darkest emotions, because I knew they always had my back. I finally didn't feel alone, I had found my tribe and was safe to express my true, weird self without any judgements. They taught me what true unconditional love is and I wouldn't have made it this far into my healing journey without them.

And then there is my one true love, my French bulldog, Havana. I never really understood what people used to say when they said their pets saved them, but this dog right here, she is a different kind of special. On the days where I was too sad to even express my emotions, she would not leave my side. She would sleep on my chest, knowing I needed some extra love. She is so intuitive, I could be silent crying with her snoring her head off next to me, and she would instantly jump out of her sleep and run over to me to give me a hug.

Being able to pour your heart out and have the love of a dog sat protecting you while you do, is a comfort you don't realise until you actually get it. If I'm having a day where my mind is in overdrive, a nice walk and a cuddle with Havana is all I need to reset me. The whole time I've been working on this book, I think she's been able to feel my emotions, as she insists on sitting on my lap whenever I am writing. Our souls are definitely connected, even the day she first came home, she was so excited and it felt like we had met before, perhaps in another life, or maybe she is someone I knew in this life, that had come back as her. What I do know though, is if I am happy Havana is happy, and if I'm not, then neither is she. She really isn't a normal dog, she has a very human spirit about her. A spirit that hugs my inner pain and tells it that it will all be ok.

And then the final big factor in my healing journey has been Reiki, which is a type of energy healing, where positive energy flows through your body, clearing out any negative energy and releasing any blockages you may have as a result of pain and trauma. Most people don't understand this part of my journey, but I've become extremely spiritual over the years, and I can honestly say Reiki has been hugely beneficial for me. I can clearly feel the effects of the energy shifting in me. I have released a lot of pain. I felt the release of years of pain I had kept in my heart. I still have a long way to go in my journey, but I have an amazing Reiki master called Carole, who is working with me to fully release my pain. Whenever I have had a session with Carole, I always feel lighter, and my mind is a lot clearer. I always feel the pain releasing from my body, as I've sat and cried it out with her, unblocking my heart chakra and embracing a sense of self love. Even Havana loves a bit of Reiki, she will lie for twenty minutes with crystals all over her chakras, snoring through her treatment. If I am aligning my chakras, of course, I have to make sure my baby's are aligned too. She is my emotional support dog, after all.

CHAPTER 35
THE TEST

With all of this work I had been putting into my healing, I finally felt strong enough to face any situation that would have previously broken me. So, when my Aunty Sarah sent me an invite to her 50th birthday party, I knew my mother would have been invited as well, but this time, I didn't freak out at the thought of seeing her. I had done enough work on myself to not let her get to me. I also had a few months to prepare for the idea of actually seeing her for the first time in almost eight years. I would have all my cousins at the party and Kiara and Kevin would be there too.

With my mother coming it also had a plus. It meant Kane would be there. After seven years of not seeing him, I was so excited about this part. The day of the party came, and even though I was anxious, I was still feeling ready for it. I headed to Laura's house, as she was doing my hair and make-up. Just as we had finished my make-up, Kiara messaged me saying that my mother had bailed on the party, apparently she was too ill and said that Kane couldn't go; despite Kiara and Kevin offering to bring him. It was a poor excuse as both my mother and Kane had been out all day, so they couldn't have been that ill. I was relieved that my mother wasn't coming, but I was devastated that I wasn't going to be able to see Kane.

Kiara sent me the screenshots of her messages with Kane where he had said he wasn't allowed to come as apparently he was "sick." He said he hasn't seen any of the family in over a year, and that our mother knew who was going to be there, so why change her mind last minute. This was typical of my mother. The amount of times I would have my hopes up for something, then at the final hour she would cancel.

I knew exactly how Kane would be feeling. He then sent another message saying:

"She said that I'm sick and if I went today, I wouldn't be well enough to go to school on Monday, and I know mummy doesn't want me to go because of Kylie, but she has always said that I can go and see her, but when I just told her that, she said that I was trying to twist her words. I'm much older now and I don't need mummy's side of her story to shape my opinion on anyone, they were both in the wrong back then, but she just hasn't moved on. It was between mummy and Kylie and I felt like I was in the middle. And yeah, sure I might not have seen Kylie for 7 years and I was nervous to see her, but if I don't have a chance to see her today, I might not see her for another 7 years. Mummy might be scared but I'm not. I was prepared for today and it's all gone to shit."

As soon as I read that message my whole aura must have changed, as Laura instantly knew something was wrong. I was holding back my tears, as I didn't want to ruin my makeup, but it felt like my heart had been ripped out all over again. The pain in my chest was unbearable and I wanted more than anything to hug my brother. All the pain I had felt over the years came flooding back, not only had that witch broken me, but the same pain I endured growing up, I could feel in my baby brother, my innocent, sweet baby brother. I wish I could have protected him from all of this, protected him from her. He didn't know the true story and I could only imagine what she must have told him, but I could still see light at the end of the tunnel, because despite all of that, he wanted to see me! I asked Kiara to screenshot a message from me and send it to him, she agreed so I wrote:

"So much has happened in the past between mother and I. He's absolutely right and that's why I had to step away. It was never because I didn't love him, but I could see that he was in the middle and I didn't want him to get hurt. But not a day has gone by in the last seven years that I haven't thought about him. However, what has got me through is knowing that he will be old enough to make his own decisions one day. And I can't wait for that day. I never want him to feel nervous or anxious about seeing me, because I am here with open arms whenever he is ready!"

As much as my heart wanted to cry, I needed to remain strong. I had been waiting for this for the last seven years and we were getting so much closer. I finally had an insight into what Kane was thinking, all these years, I had questioned if he even wanted a relationship with me again. This was clarity that one day, I would have my baby back. Even though he was now 15 years old, in my head he is still that 7 year old little boy. So, he will always be a baby in my eyes.

After sending the message, I composed myself and tried to put it to the back of my mind, so I wouldn't ruin my evening. It was actually nice to be able to enjoy the party without the worry of an abundant amount of death stares from my mother. Towards the end of the evening, I was sat with Kevin discussing what had happened earlier with Kane. He told me that Kane had never expressed his feelings towards me, but that now he knows how important it was for him to see me, he was going to figure out a way to reunite us.

I told him how much that would mean to me, and then started to speak to Kevin about everything that had happened between my mother and I. As transparent as Kiara and I were with what had happened in the past, Kevin and I had never really spoken about it. I feel like when my mother kicked me out the first time, she had manipulated my relationship with Kevin and we had grown apart, so it never really felt right to bring it up with him. I didn't know where he sat with regards to the whole situation, and as strongly as I felt about my mother, I have never and will never try to influence how my siblings feel about her. It is their prerogative to decide how they deal with her. Yet, for some reason, it felt right to bring it up now.

I turned to Kevin and said, "We've never spoken about this before, but a lot went down between mum and me, a lot you don't even know about, but I never want you to think that it was an easy decision for me to walk away from you."

He turned back to me. "I know more than you realise, I did come across your blog a few years back, and when I read it I had a panic attack. I know it's not your fault, we all have our issues as a result of her and we have to try and stop her having the same effect on Kane."

At this point, all the emotions of the evening came to the surface. I could no longer hold them in, floods of tears poured down my face, sat in the corner of the party, everyone dancing around us oblivious. "I can't tell you how much it means to me to hear you say this, I've worried for years that you would hate me for leaving, but it breaks my heart to know how much you have been affected by this too. I never wanted anyone to have that reaction to my blog, but it honestly was the hardest thing I've ever done in my life walking away from you all, I'm sorry."

Kiara suddenly noticed the intensity of the conversation and came running over. The three of us stood crying together, whilst Kiara's boyfriend Jason shielded us from the crowd, ensuring no one interrupted this very needed moment. They both promised me that they were going to make this better and assured me they had my back. If you knew how many years, I had been waiting to hear those words! The moment I realised, they didn't hate me for leaving, they didn't judge me, they understood. Those words right there fixed a little part of my heart that evening. And for the first time in years we felt reunited. I had longed for this moment, the only piece missing now was Kane, but if having this heart to heart had taught me anything, it was that everything was going to be okay from here.

The morning after the party, I was telling Arianna what happened. She was fuming and starting plotting ways she could go and get back at my mother for me. I was trying to tell her it wasn't about her anymore and that she was an irrelevant part of the story now, yet her fiery Italian side was not backing down, and I became really overwhelmed. I loved her so much for having my back the way she did, but in that moment, I didn't have the fight in me, I just needed a hug. I was emotionally and mentally exhausted. Everything from the previous day had been a lot to deal with. So, I left her ranting and went to have a shower, so I could just cry and process everything. I cried my eyes out in that shower, how after all these years, after all the work I had done healing, *how was this woman still getting to me like this?* Yes, I was healing. I thought I had healed, but you are never fully healed. I am always going to have days that literally feel like I've been smacked in the face with an iron rod. And that was okay.

I had my moment and I carried on, and picked up when I had left off. This was how I knew I have come a long way in my healing journey. It's not about not having a breakdown, it's about how long it takes you to get back up after. And I was getting up a lot quicker than I would have at the beginning of this journey.

Christmas was now quickly approaching, and by now you should know how this time of the year made me feel. I had just moved to my new home and had popped to the shops to get a few essentials, when I was walking through the shopping centre, I noticed someone who looked like Kiara, as I got closer I realised it was her, she was with someone, my eyesight is terrible when I'm not wearing my glasses, so it wasn't until I got closer that I realised, she was with Kane. My heart almost skipped a beat. I couldn't believe it.

"Kiara!" I shouted with excitement. They turned around and I was stood face to face, with my not so little brother. I couldn't believe it, in all these years, we had never bumped into each other. Kane and I were both just stood there grinning ear to ear, before I gave him a huge hug. It felt like all my Christmas' had come at once. My sister did most of the talking, as I think I was too in awe to speak. Kane and I continued to just smile at each other, my cheeks were hurting from the constant grin, but I couldn't stop it. I walked them to the train station and gave Kane another hug, telling him that I hoped to see him soon.

I walked home on cloud nine, I don't even think I got what I went to the shops for. This was the best Christmas present I could have asked for, it was like a confirmation from the Universe, to let me know I was on the right path and to remind me of my end result. Remind me of my 'Why.' Being reunited with ALL of my siblings.

I can't tell you how the story ends, because my story is a never ending one, but I have hope, that I know the next chapter, until then I will continue on with my healing journey, becoming the best version of myself for my siblings.

I've accepted that it's okay if I'm not feeling positive every day, that doesn't mean that I've failed. I'm still human. I've accepted that it's okay if I want to spend an entire day in bed crying. It doesn't mean I am weak. Sometimes I just need some processing time. I'm not ashamed to admit that anymore. I spent my entire life living on edge, so getting my nervous system back to a sense of calm, is a work in progress.

I am a work in progress. And I'm okay with that. If my 10-year-old self could see me now, I know she would be proud. I have become the person I needed when I was growing up, and I can't wait to see her continue to grow. For anyone out there that can relate to my story in the slightest. Don't give up, there is a way out and you can turn things around.

You are not alone and you never will be xxx.

Printed in Great Britain
by Amazon